I Will Remain

MJ Peiffer
7/24/2014

Copyright…
Library of Congress
ISBN: 0578164124

Table of Contents

	Pg.
1. Waiting	3
2. Photos	10
3. Not Forgotten	13
4. Perspective	17
5. Understanding	20
6. Jeff	25
7. The Lily	36
8. Unrecognizable	40
9. Worry	48
10. Red	50
11. Beginning	56
12. Hope	60
13. Failure	67
14. Tears	69
15. Exhaustion	73
16. Relief	78
17. In Kind	83
18. Certainty	87
19. Impending	92
20. Determination	95
21. Struck	97
22. Inevitability	100
23. Timing	108
24. Coincidences?	113
25. Not at all	118
26. Please Don't	124
27. The Facts	127
28. Tomorrow	131
29. Now what?	136
30. Just unfair	140
31. Endings	144
32. Running	151

33. Decisions	153
34. Signs	159
35. Basic Addition	161
36. Bait	165
37. Family	168

-1-
Waiting

"She is going to die."

"She is going to die and I can't do anything about it." Those are the thoughts Marcus is raging against inside his head as he sits defeated, with his head in his hands in the Faith General ICU waiting room.

Marcus has a headache and is beginning to lose confidence in both the hopeful outcome of the diagnosis and the hospital staff themselves, even as he wars to be positive and prays silently. He has been waiting four hours in a waiting room full of sepulchral family members to find out if his sister Lauren is going to live.

Marcus is irritable, hungry and extremely exhausted after his ten hour drive from Las Vegas to San Francisco. It was two twelve in the morning when he received the call from Kevin, his brother in law. Less than twenty-four hours ago, the timber of Kevin's voice had instantly chilled Marcus awake.

Marcus and Kevin had rarely spoken before. Prior to that call they had exchanged no more than ten sentences between them. If Marcus were asked honestly, he would say that he doesn't even like Kevin.

After that call however, Marcus would, at very least, say he is certain that Kevin truly loves Lauren. That vastly improves Kevin in his eyes, regardless of actual personality. Marcus could hear the terror, worry and strain in every word as Kevin had said to him. "The doctors don't think she is going to make it, they said to notify the family. Her kidneys are failing from the toxic amount of antibiotics in her system needed to fight the infection," sounding as though he had memorized those phrases verbatim from the doctors.

Marcus hadn't spoken to his older sister Lauren in at least a year because they had had a falling out over Marcus's harsh and unwanted opinions of Lauren's choices in regards to her son Jeff. Jeff was five when Lauren married Kevin. Jeff is Marcus's favorite person in the world and had felt as though Lauren's prior boyfriend and likely Kevin too, were at minimum, border-line abusive with Jeff.

Jeff has never said it, but Marcus knows verbal abuse when he witnesses it. Marcus hates how Kevin speaks to Jeff. Every word Kevin says to Jeff is heavily laced with resentment and burden.

Lauren always acts like she doesn't hear it and never defends Jeff in Marcus's presence. Marcus rarely speaks to Lauren anymore because of that disregard and her proclivity to treat her daughter much better than she treats Jeff. Lauren's daughter Cassie is only three. Marcus can't see Cassie growing up into anything other than the smart mouth, disrespectful, entitled spawn that troll the malls in droves. She is terribly spoiled but she is *incredibly* cute, Marcus smiles at the recollection of Cassie's little face.

In light of current circumstances, Marcus can't help but think of how tragic it would be for Cassie to grow up without a mother. Praying silently, Marcus entreats God on Laurens behalf. "I promise you can take any blessings I may have earned and give them all to Lauren and her family. Please let her make it through this, for Jeff's sake, for Cassie's, for Kevin, and even for me. I don't know what to do about Jeff if she doesn't make it through God. Please in your son's name, Jesus. Christ, Amen." Marcus finishes in a rushed whisper.

Unaware that he had closed them, he opens his eyes, surveying the room. He is astonished to see so many faces that he knows and many that he knows he should know but can't quite place. They all bear a family resemblance to his mother's side of the family. Lauren was always much more involved with that part of the family than he had been. Lauren stayed with the sisters and brothers of their mother as a child but he had not.

Lauren and Marcus were raised by their father predominantly because their mother had been extremely physically abusive. Their father Kellan had fought for two years for custody of the two children and finally won. It was unheard of at that time for a single man to get sole custody of two children, especially considering that one of them was not his own.

To be raised by Kellan meant he had been reared with an unwavering sense of devotion to all children. Lauren had not even been Kellan's child. Kellan adopted Lauren when he married their mother and treated Lauren and Marcus exactly the same as Marcus saw it. Lauren had always grown up feeling hard done by. In Marcus's opinion Lauren's resentment of Kellan was a rotten seed planted in her mind by their mother Diane.

It is mostly Diane's family that occupies the waiting room, Kellan doesn't have much family.

Diane's two brothers and two sisters have always known her to be an unworthy mother. There had been times before Diane met Kellan that she would drop Lauren off to be "babysat" and wouldn't return for her daughter for several months at a time.

Lauren is closely bonded to their Uncle Ricky, and Aunt Alice, because they had taken it in turns to raise Lauren for portions of her life. Prior to Kellan adopting her, Lauren had been shunted from relative to relative over the years. Marrying Kellan McGregor had stabilized Diane to some degree.

Marcus has always loved his big sister even when she was cold and distant to him. Marcus also knows that Kellan has always loved Lauren too. "I wish she could just stop keeping him at a distance and allow him to love her." Marcus thinks, allowing his mind to wander as he vaguely wonders what happened to his Uncle Philip whom he had met only once in his life, and his Aunt Connie whom he has no recollection of at all. *Lauren would know.*

As Marcus is thinking, he looks down the hospital hallway to the Intensive Care Unit room where Lauren is now unconscious and fighting for her life.

From the fifty foot distance to Lauren's room Marcus can see Kellan exiting the glass barricade. Kellan takes two staggering steps and falls to his knees, in tears, begging God to take him instead of Lauren. Kellan's forehead is bowed so low that his dishwater blonde hair dangles centimeters above his strong capable hands, splayed on the sterile hospital tiles. Marcus wishes someone had gotten that on camera so he could show it to Lauren if she recovers. "If" seemed so harsh of a word under the circumstances. Marcus grits his teeth considering what the doctors had explained to the room full of expectant family four hours ago.

"Lauren is dying from the flesh eating strain of Streptococcus that we suspect had entered into her body through her eye only two days ago. Her immune system just can't fight it off fast enough. I am sorry." Dr. Mashhad had stated in her formal and clipped tone. That statement concurred with what Kevin had told Marcus.

Over the phone, Kevin had explained that Lauren had come home two days before complaining that her eye hurt, within a couple hours it had swollen shut, then her face and neck swelled as the bacteria traveled through her body, then on to her bloodstream and organs. This strain of strep is rare, fast acting and highly aggressive. The doctors thought she may have been exposed to it while shaking hands with someone on one of the tours she gave at work. All she would have to of done was touch her eye for it to transfer.

It all sounded so surreal to Marcus, something out of a bad horror flick. He still couldn't wrap his mind around it, but his heart was feeling the pain and fear of reality. Marcus feels as though he hasn't taken a complete breath since he got the call from Kevin. *Worry is the heaviest weight,* Marcus realizes.

Although he feels like he barely knows any of them, Marcus is moved by the show of concern by these estranged family members. They were never part of his life, with one exception. His stoic and brusque Grandfather, Luis Miguel Castillo, his mother's father.

Luis is the most aged and yet dominant face in the room. He has the shriveled and hobbled look of the elderly as he slumps in his chair against the wall, fading in and out of sleep. Marcus absorbs the comportment of the man as though he is of no relation to him. Remembering that Luis is eighty-two years old, Marcus gathers the memories of his Grandfather in his mind. Flipping through them like a mental photo album.

Marcus feels disconnected from Luis after so many years. Marcus had not seen Luis since his freshman year in college. Luis had come to watch Marcus play his first scrimmage basketball game for the University of Wyoming. Marcus had gotten a full ride scholarship to play basketball for the Cowboys but had not really wanted to go to school in the back hills of Wyoming.

In his youth, Luis had once been an English professor at U.W. and had coached basketball for them. Luis had recently settled back in Wyoming shortly after his wife died. Marcus recalls that Luis had been less than positive about Marcus's performance although Marcus had ended up being named MVP of the tournament. Luis had critiqued every single motion of Marcus's layup as though Marcus were the cogs of a watch that told correct time but did not run as smoothly as it could have. Luis had only constructive criticism; no praise was ever known to come from his mouth. Marcus remembers how after listening to Luis deconstruct his skill level Marcus had walked away muttering, "Wow, I guess Uncle Phil was right. Nothing is ever good enough."

Marcus had minimal childhood memories of Luis as his mother's parents weren't exactly what one would consider involved Grandparents. He remembered funny things mostly from when his grandmother Janie had been alive. Marcus smiles as the memory of "Grandpa Surprise" surfaces. The concoction was fed to him and Lauren one morning after sleeping on his grandparent's living room floor.

Grandpa surprise was a combined variety of many different cereals that Luis liked and had eaten all but the dregs of. As with many people who had lived through World War II and The Great Depression, Luis never wasted food. Never a crumb was thrown away. So the vestiges of the multiple cereals were combined into one bag until Luis had enough left over crumbs to make into a bowlful.

Marcus could now understand where his mother got her obsessively frugal nature. It had never been pleasant to dress for school when his parents had been married. His Father had worked sixteen hour days in the Coal Mines of Colorado and had left every detail of the homemaking to Diane. Diane never worked outside of their home for the fifteen years that she was dating and married to Kellan. Kellan had become the provider for Diane and Lauren for three years before they were married. Kellan had saved Diane and Lauren from Diane's first husband; an alarmingly disturbed combat medic that had done three tours in the worst parts of the Viet Nam war zone. Marcus knew of his mother's first husband only from the bits of conversation he had overheard between his mother and her friends over the years.

Now at twenty-six years old, Marcus could recognize the signs in those conversations, of what his mother had admitted to him two years ago. "I never loved your Father Marcus." Diane had said without apology. Marcus had felt like someone had punched him in his temple.

"Then why did you marry him Mom? You should never have had me. That is a horrible thing to do."

"Because he loved me, and I had a daughter to take care of. What was I supposed to do?" was her dower response.

"You were supposed to get a job and support Lauren and yourself until you found a man that you wanted to make happy, instead you had me, trapped him and made him miserable for taking care of you." Marcus had said with all the venom he felt she had poisoned them with their entire lives.

"Oh, you are young, what do you know? It was a different time. I did what I needed to do." Diane had said and waved him away like he was a worrisome insect buzzing about her head.

Marcus realized in that moment that he didn't like his mother. He didn't hate her. He acknowledged his obligatory concern for her as the woman who had given him life, but she had broken any true affection he had ever had for her that day.

Marcus often pondered the effect his parent's relationship would have on him as he attempted to navigate the adult world of relationships, love and commitment. He often told people that he had no chance at having a healthy adult relationship because he had never witnessed one. It was just not the knowledge or skill set that he possessed.

That is not entirely true as Marcus knows. Kellan had given Marcus some sound advice where women were concerned but Marcus had never met a woman he felt motivated to make a real effort with. No one had ever "*Struck*" him as Kellan had said would one day happen.

Kellan had told Marcus over and over again since Marcus had been fourteen years old. "One day son, you will look at some girl, your world will shift and every other girl will fade away. No other girl will hold as much fascination for you as *that* girl. They can be prettier than she is, they can be smarter or have more in common with you but none of that will matter. When you find that one there will be no other *one* for you… and when you do meet her… Work hard for her, to get her and once you get her, work every day to keep her. Ruin her with kindness so that no other man will have a hope of turning her head."

Marcus had for years dismissed Kellan's tipsy ranting's, yet couldn't help but notice all through High School and College how everyone seemed to fall in love but him. Love as a topic had become a curious affliction that Marcus seemed immune to. Once he had even dated a tall, powerful and beautiful volleyball player. For two years in College he had attempted to see if he could one day *find* himself in love since it hadn't struck him. He took Kellan's further advice and had treated Rowan "How you want your sister to be treated."

After two years of ease and comfort Rowan had come to Marcus and asked him, "Marc, I am not *the one* for you am I?"

Marcus had just stared at her blankly because he liked Rowan, appreciated her and enjoyed sex with her, but he knew that he never missed her when she was on her game trips, never throbbed for her, she just fit into his life and didn't make it any harder, so he kept her, hoping he would wake up one day ravenous for her, heart and soul.

"Come on Marc, we have a great time, we are comfortable but we aren't crazy in love are we?" Rowan had pressed.

"No, I don't think so." Marcus had admitted. Rowan had nodded and settled into the crook of his arm on the couch next to him. They had sat and eaten their pizza, watched a movie, had sex then went to bed. In the morning Marcus had woken up and noticed that all of Rowan's accumulated bathroom products were gone. They never spoke privately again but were perfectly friendly to each other when they saw each other in social gatherings. Marcus had noted that Rowan never seemed particularly broken up about their split so he felt ok with it. He never wanted to hurt her and felt relief that she hadn't been.

-2-
Photos

Marcus is watching Kellan pull himself off the hospital floor and collect himself as three nurses' swarm around him offering aid and condolences. Marcus smiles. Hopefully Kellan will get a date out of this whole mess. That would be an upside.

Marcus often worries about his father's solitude. He knows that Kellan has dated recently but also knows that nothing has gotten serious. Marcus calls Kellan at least once a month just to check in and see if his Father needs anything. Kellan and Marcus had a good friendship where Kellan would often seem to forget that Marcus is his son and would over share details from time to time. Kellan is a good man and father but had always been a bit brusque and unapproachable. He wasn't the kind of father that you could turn to for emotional support or to confide in. He would hug his children upon greeting and when parting company but wasn't truly demonstrative or affectionate. Although he was playful, he wasn't the Father that would throw a birthday party for Marcus or Lauren but would call each child on the other's birthday.

Marcus had always wished his mother had been more present because there had been many times when he was young that he had wished he had a shoulder to cry on or to just be held and cuddled like he had seen other mothers do to his friends.

Lauren, like their mother, was not affectionate either. Marcus had long ago admitted that *he* was the one in the family that had the soft heart and sweet demeanor.

His great Aunt Moray, Kellan's mother's sister had confided to Marcus once that he had been the same kind of boy Kellan had been. Kellan was once, openly affectionate and kind as a child but his parents had broken him of that and "toughened him up" by the time Kellan had reached young adulthood.

Marcus had felt compassion for his father and understood him just a little more after Moray had explained to him what his Grandparents had been like. They had sounded efficient and responsible but not loving or nurturing by any standard. Marcus had made the connection in his mind that Kellan on some level had married a version of his own mother. A realization that had made Marcus determined to break that cycle.

Marcus wants a woman who is strong but nurturing and soft in her heart and soul. A romantic, artistic and poetic woman who can make Marcus see the blazing sunset when he is too deep in his head to notice on his own. He wants a woman that blazes with the passion of life and for him. Marcus wants to blaze for someone as Kellan had described.

That thought jostles something free from Marcus's subconscious. He frowns scouring his mind for the connection he knew was just beyond full comprehension. His gaze slid from face to face in the room, as he strained to make the synapsis complete. Finally his eyes light on the face of his Grandfather Luis. The memory he had been searching for surfaces as he studies Luis speculatively.

Marcus had been helping his mother pack up some of her mother's possessions. Diane had been shooting small facts to Marcus as she wrapped large gaudy pieces of costume jewelry into separate velvet bags. "This one was not my mother's originally; it had been her mother's from when she had been a Ziegfeld Girl."

Marcus had not really cared but had been bored so had asked just to keep up conversation, "What is a Ziegfeld Girl?"

"Well, here you go, see…My grandmother." Diane had handed Marcus a stack of old ornately carved picture frames. The pictures were old and yellowed but he could see they had once been black and white photos of a woman in an enormous headdress. Layers upon layers of feathers arranged high on her head attached to a jeweled cap that fitted to her head. The entire headdress must have been half as tall as the woman was. She wasn't thin and frail like the models that Marcus saw in the magazines at the grocery store. She looked big chested with an unnaturally small waist and wide hips. He remembered thinking that she looked like a statue in a museum, with her stiffly erect posture and expressionless face. She wasn't pretty but he could see a definite resemblance to Diane. Marcus had said half of what he had been thinking. "She looks like you a little bit huh mom?" Diane gave a dismissive shrug but Marcus had seen her brow furrow.

"This," Diane had said as she took the first frame and packed it in a box, tapping on the glass of the frame now facing Marcus from the stack, "is your grandmother, my mommy. She was very beautiful wasn't she?"

Marcus had looked at the faded color picture and had been stunned. Even at nine years old Marcus could recognize that his grandmother had been truly beautiful. She stood erect in a dark green Army uniform. An odd little cap on her pitch black rolled hair that perfectly framed her face. Perfectly manicured eyebrows set in arches above black lined eyes thick with long lashes that looked like fans were framing large liquid dark eyes, in contrast to her porcelain white skin. Her lips were full and red. Marcus inhaled deeply, "*This* is Grandma? She looks just like Snow White. She was *really* pretty."

Marcus continued to look through the frames, all of which were pictures of Janie. Some were professional pictures of her in dirty shapeless coveralls that did not hide her curvy body, hair tied back from her face in a red patterned handkerchief, black greasy smudges on her khaki outfit and on her shining face. Marcus asked "What is this outfit mom?"

Diane had smiled. "Your grandmother was a pin-up girl while she was in the Army with your Grandpa. She had been a B-1 Bomber mechanic and that was her outfit that she had to wear to fix the airplane engines. I never saw her like that. I was born after she became a teacher. I always saw her in suits. But even dirty she was pretty huh?" Marcus could see the pride shining in his mother's eyes. "Grandma ended up becoming a Ziegfeld girl too right before she married Grandpa." Appraising his mother's face he looked for Diane's resemblance to her mother. He didn't see it. Nine year old Marcus looked back into the frame and thought about how cool it was that the woman in the photo had fixed plane engines.

Looking up to the mechanical hospital grade bed in his grandparents bedroom he couldn't put this beautiful woman together with the frizzy, white haired, woman that said her prayers many times a day and looked down her nose at him as though he were something dirty and unkempt. She had been nearly as big the bed she had been confined to for the five years he had known her. He couldn't assign the glamorous young woman in the pictures with the title of grandmother. He also could not imagine that the obese, mean natured, invalid in the bed before him could be the same woman that was impressive and brave enough to be in the Army fixing airplanes. None of those images fit together for him.

The last frame in the stack was a photo of his grandmother holding a curly haired baby in a white pinafore, standing next to an extremely thin, much darker complexion man. Marcus had recognized the features of his grandfather. Smooth with youth and vibrancy, his eyes sparked from the monochromatic photo in the same way they still sparked at Marcus now, almost intimidatingly.

In that moment of recollection Marcus wishes he had known his grandmother better before she had died four years before this dismal day in Faith General.

-3-
Not Forgotten

Marcus surfaces from the memory to look up at Luis. Luis is looking back at him with a penetrating stare. Marcus has the irrationally guilty feeling of having spoken behind someone's back. Luis does not break the eye contact; he does not smile at Marcus or entreat him in any way. Marcus watches until the challenging light fades from Luis's eyes an increment. Almost without his own knowledge Marcus stands and walks the three steps to his Grandfather and sits down next to him.

Luis does not speak. Marcus feels slightly uneasy but can feel his mouth open and words come out. The instant his sentence has begun his mind catches up to his mouth and he inwardly cringes. What a horrible way to start a conversation he thinks as he hears himself say. "Grandpa, are you happy?"

Luis looks at him incredulously. "What?" The deep, slightly accented voice of the young powerful man in the photo says from between the lips of this withered old man. "Of course I am not happy."

"Is there anything I can get you? Anything I can do to make you more comfortable?" Marcus offers.

"Can you go get my best friend?" Luis's eyes roll back in his head, closed with a look of longing that makes him seem years younger. Marcus doesn't know what Luis is talking about so he just sits silently and waits. Luis opens one eye and looks slyly out of the corner of it as though spying on his grandson.

Marcus looks into that eye; Luis lifts his head and reaches into the fanny pack at his waist that Marcus had not noticed. Marcus smiles and laughs inwardly at the use of such an antiquated fashion trend. Old people are so strange and eccentric Marcus thinks to himself.

Luis removes a Velcro Army green wallet that has a gold embroidered patch of staff sergeant rank super glued to the outside of the adhesive flap. Thumbing past all of the photos captured within the plastic sheaves to the hidden pocket under the ID window, Luis removes a worn picture that is yellowing around the edges. On the back, there is something written in faded but scrawling penmanship. Luis hands the photo to Marcus facedown. "Here she is. I miss her every day." Marcus turns the laminated photo over in his hands; Janie 1947, Basic Training, the ink states. It is the same picture of his Grandmother in her Army Dress greens, beautiful in her fitted pencil skirt and black patent leather baby doll pumps, rosy lips and a mysteriously look of dignified intensity that Marcus had missed as a boy.

Marcus doesn't know why the simple act of carrying a photo around for over half a century, four years of which the person in the photo had been dead, is so moving that his throat constricts tightly. It takes a few moments before Marcus can speak. His voice sounds thick and rugged as he asks. "Still grandpa? You are in love with her still?"

Luis looks at Marcus full in the face, his yellowed scared iris's trap Marcus from behind unspent tears. "Always, I remain in love with her. I will remain so until I die maybe even after that. Death is no larger a gap than we have been separated by before. I will find her again." Luis takes the photo back from Marcus and looks intently into Janie's face. A wrinkled road map of leathered hand presses the photo to his chest, his head rocks back and settles on the wall. Luis closes his eyes and a single tear slowly breaks free of the thin lashes of the eye closest to Marcus.

Marcus is uncomfortable and feels as though he is an interloper in the forest of Luis's memories. Not wanting to intrude he sits silently next to Luis and watches the clock tick by. Several minutes pass without a sound from anyone in the room. The central air whirs to life, moving the stagnant air of the small room just enough to make people stand or shift. It has been seven hours since any hospital staff had spoken to the family.

Marcus begins to think about Lauren again and tells himself it can't be a good sign that they haven't heard anything yet. Kellan enters the room and nods in Marcus's direction.

Kellan strides over to Luis and extends his hand, offering to shake. "It is good to see you old man. How are you?" Kellan says with a friendly air that doesn't quite rate as genuine, more along the lines of polite obligation.

Marcus has always known that his Mother's parents did not care for his father. That was obvious. Marcus had always thought it was unfair. As a result his heart had hardened towards his grandparents when he was a child.

Luis looks with obvious disdain at Kellan's extended hand. He does not accept the gesture but looks at Kellan's frozen grin and states plainly. "I am fine. Thank you." Kellan drops his hand. Marcus stands up to hug his father. Kellan returns the hug looking into Marcus's eyes. Kellan's eyes are filled with pain and worry.

"She doesn't even look like herself, I couldn't stay in there. The only recognizable feature is her gorgeous black hair. I remember how angry I was when your mother had cut it all off like a little boy when she was ten. You don't remember that do you? You were only five." Kellan says softly just to Marcus.

Marcus shakes his head confirming that he does not remember. "I will go in in a few minutes. I want to wait to hear what the Doctors say." Kellan excuses himself to go to the restroom.

Marcus is angry at the snub that Luis had just delivered to his father. *Cantankerous old man*, Marcus thinks to himself. Marcus knows that Luis has a bias opinion of Kellan due to the complaints and constant berating his mother had always heaped upon Kellan's shoulders when speaking to her family. She never once had said anything nice about Kellan to any of her family in the many long distance phone calls that Kellan ended up paying for. In light of Diane's recent admission he felt he had to finally stick up for his father. His mother's family should know how Diane had tortured Kellan with constant emasculating discontent.

Marcus waits until he hears the bathroom door close behind Kellan before he says, "She never loved him you know? She told me so, to my face." Marcus says with a hard edge to his voice and loud enough for everyone in the room to hear. All eyes turn to Marcus but he does not see. His head is back against the wall eyes closed just like Luis's had been prior to Kellan's entrance.

Marcus opens his eyes and lifts his head to look at his grandfather. Luis frowns asking, "Who are you talking about child?"

"Diane. My mother." Marcus waits for this to sink in. When no one responds he continues. "She told me to my face two years ago that she never loved my father, she only married him because he wanted to take care of her."

Luis glares at Marcus and sits up a little straighter in his chair turning a few degrees to face Marcus. "How could she love him? He is not a good person. He was not good to her. He is not a good man." Marcus sits forward, leaning his elbows on his knees, clasping his hands in anger in front of his face, he glares back at the elderly man.

"I mean no disrespect Grandfather but you don't know my father, you only know what my mother has told you and witnessed what he was like when you visited and ganged up on him. I remember the arguments. I remember thinking it wasn't nice when I was a kid and now as an adult I know that no man should have to endure that treatment under his own roof. My father loved my mother and still does, even though she was horrible to him and to us; he loved her anyway. That is why he hates her now."

Luis scoffed loudly. "You young people talk about love like you know. You don't know. You don't have to work for anything or live through anything rough to even understand what love is. You are a baby, barely alive, what have you lived through? What do you know of love?"

"Nothing Grandfather, I know *nothing* of love because my parents were a terrible example. I know nothing of love, because my mother knew nothing of love." Marcus stands up intent on leaving the room but turns and locks eyes with his grandfather. "I do know that my mother wasn't a good person. She abused Lauren and me physically and my father emotionally my entire childhood until my *father*," Marcus realizes he yelled the last word and calms. "Took us away from her. I know that I am a good and kind person because *he* raised me." Marcus lifts his arm, finger pointing in the direction his father had exited down the hall. "My mother, your daughter cannot take any credit for that. Who would take credit for her, how she turned out?"

Marcus looked at every adult in the room, pinning them with his eyes. One by one they lower their gaze. Marcus turns his back to the room, "I also know Lauren isn't even his but *he* is here and Diane is not. In fact, none of you would even know Lauren if Diane hadn't dumped her on all of you off and on until my Father took them in… so none of you would be here either."

Marcus walks away, needing to breathe fresh air; he stalks angrily down the hall and out the automatic doors. Marcus doesn't envy the looks his father is going to get from his mother's hot blooded family upon his return from the restroom but someone should tell them about themselves for once.

-4-
Perspective

Marcus is angry; angry that his grandfather had disrespected Kellan, angry that no one was fair or objective enough to see past Diane's poisonous negativity about Kellan, angry that they couldn't admit that Diane was a terrible mother and wife, angry that Lauren is dying and angry with himself for feeling properly ashamed that he had just lost his temper in a room full of his elders. No matter that they deserve the same disrespect they had always treated his father with. Breathing in long deep breaths to lower his elevated heart rate he paces in front of the entrance. Allowing the cool night air to calm him he takes a seat on an iron bench meant for smokers, not willing to go back in to face them while he is angry.

Marcus is enjoying a small moment of vindictive pleasure imagining that Luis felt the right amount of shame for having always thought badly of Kellan. The more reasonable part of Marcus told him that scenario is highly unlikely.

"You know, that was quite a brave little speech for a twenty-six year old." Diane's younger sister Alice says softly as she too sits on the bench Marcus is occupying. Marcus says nothing, unsure if she was mocking him, baiting him or just being condescending, but dually surprised that she knows his age. Alice continues. "Quite brave of you to have not sugar coated that for Dad. He needs to hear it. Your grandparents have always lived self-righteously in their own built up moral high ground, while they refuse to see their own short comings." Marcus listens intently feeling it would be churlish to confirm her statements.

Alice has such a similar face to Diane's that it is somewhat disconcerting. Her face is broader and much darker in complexion with slightly greying teeth to match her salt and pepper hair that falls to her shoulders. Marcus can see that she is the only female in her family that has the same teak colored complexion as Luis. Her two sisters were pale with freckles. All five of Luis's children have the intensely black colored cornea that is inseparable from the iris, just as Luis has.

Looking into Alice's face is like staring down his mother with a deep tan. Marcus shakes his head to clear the misconception.

Alice clears her throat, a dry raspy sound. "Your mother was not a good mother Marcus. We all know that. Your Father has turned out to be a better man than any of us thought he was. Granted our opinions were colored by the horror stories Diane told us about him. Your parents are just two people who brought out the turpitude in each other. They should never have been together." Alice adjusts her patchwork chenille shawl, grasping it closer to her age rounded shoulders. Marcus is impacted by how frail and old she looks, nearly as old as her own father. Lauren had always spoken of how much of a rebel, hippy that Aunt Alice is. Marcus smiles at her as best he can with his lips pursed so tightly.

"Many men have loved your mother and she has only loved the one, Lauren's father, but in the end, she tortured him just as she tortured every man… with his own love. It is unfortunate your father had to be one of the men who really loved her. Too few people know what love is, fewer know *how* to love and even fewer still know how to *be* loved." Alice sighs heavily as though those words had been a weighty burden she was finally able to lay down. Her shoulder length hair tosses back and forth behind her head as the breeze lures it away from her face. Her strong profile looks troubled.

"You think you don't know anything about love because your parents didn't give you an example, but I am here to tell you, that can't be the case. We all must learn to love as best we know how in our own way." Alice rests her hand on top of the hand Marcus has wrapped around the edge of the iron bench between them. She wraps her fingers around and between his, holding tight as though securing his hand to the bench for safety. Marcus looks up at her. She is not looking at him. She is staring out across the circle of lawn in the center of the hospital drive, where the Flag pole waves slightly as the Flag billows in the breeze.

"My parents, your grandparents have an incredible love story, they loved each other more deeply than any character in any love story ever told, and none of us seem to know how to love like that. We had a great example of a deep loving relationship right in front of us our whole lives and all of us are screwed up and none of the five of us have a healthy marriage." She frowns looking down at her feet, then up to Marcus's face. Marcus can see a deep sadness etched in every wrinkle and line of his Aunts face. She suddenly seems so old and so young in her pain that she appears to be ageless and beautiful in the most heartbreaking way Marcus has ever witnessed. The softness in his aunt's face is what separates her from his mother. Aunt Alice is a handsome woman and looks every bit, part of the proud, strong people who's DNA she shared in the arching line of her cheekbones and the drooping fullness of her bottom lip. He can, in this forlorn moment see her atop a cliff the wind blowing her long black mane of hair in the wind as he always imagined the beautiful Aztec women had hundreds of years ago. Her low voice brings him back to reality.

"The best advice I can give you in your youth is; to love hard and as long as you can until you get your heart broken… then do it again… and again until you find someone who loves you exactly the way you need to be loved, then find out what makes her *feel* loved and do exactly whatever that is. Make someone happy because it makes you happy and love for no other reason than that. Don't ever be afraid to get hurt, you will always get over it. Have no pride when someone is more important to you than that pride. Those are all the things I messed up when I was young and the reason I am alone now. There is always a possibility of enduring happiness and happiness is all you deserve to get, if you have it, do whatever you have to do to keep it." Alice stands up abruptly and walks back to the front doors. From over his shoulder Marcus can hear her call, "Oh and find someone who has your same work ethic in a relationship, no matter how good or bad yours is. Then at least when you inevitably fail each other you will understand each other." Her long skirts, hair and shawl billow around her like the smoke of a magician as she disappears behind the tinted glass doors.

Marcus feels as though he asked for a glass of water and someone threw him in a swimming pool. "Now drink." He says sarcastically to himself. He also wishes he had been given a chance to record that. It sounded like the wisest thing anyone had ever said to him. When his brain is no longer the consistency of oatmeal, he will attempt to decipher as much of that speech as he can.

Marcus removes a napkin from his pocket and writes down as much of Alice's advice as he can remember. He will ask her to fill in the holes later.

-5-
Understanding

Marcus looks at his watch. It has been another hour since he had come outside for some air. He is calm now and feels it is safe to return to the waiting room. He is considering going back to check with the nurses' station about visiting Lauren, when the soft scuff of his father's snake skin, leather soled cowboy boots attracts his attention. Marcus would know that sound anywhere. It is as familiar to him as his own face. He doesn't turn to greet his father, knowing Kellan may just have needed some air as well and not wanting to interrupt Kellan's thoughts.

Marcus understands his father; he always has in most ways. There are few areas concerning Diane that Marcus does not understand but Marcus has always attributed those gaps to his lack of experience in the relationship department. Marcus has never understood why Kellan had stayed with Diane for so long or why he let her talk down to him. When Marcus was young he would sometimes think his father needed to stick up for himself but at other times he could see how it made Kellan so tired to fight her.

Marcus can remember how it was between his parents when he was little, so little he doesn't remember his exact age, only that he wasn't yet in school. Marcus has one memory of his mother sitting on the couch with her feet up on the table when Kellan had come in and sat in Diane's lap with his back to her, straddling her extended legs. Kellan then bent over and nibbled Diane's exposed knees, effectively pinning her so that she could not fight off Kellan's tickling bites. Diane shrieked and begged for Kellan to stop, laughing until she couldn't breathe. Only when she was breathless had Kellan released her and turned to hug and kiss her all over her face.

Marcus has only that one good memory of his parents playing and acting as though they liked and loved each other. By the time he was in Kindergarten he can remember knowing that his parents were miserable and that he was terrified of his mother. By second grade Marcus can remember walking home every day from school wondering what he will have done to incite Diane's wrath and how bad his beating was going to be. It was never a question of *if* he was going to be hit every day, but *for what*?

Now as an adult he can't help think how pitiful it is for an eight year old to be resigned to abuse like that. He vowed to never have a child with a woman that wasn't soft and nurturing and who really wanted children. Marcus had never been told Diane didn't want children but he knew that she resented having had them and had always felt held back from a different life by having them.

Motion in the corner of his eye makes Marcus turn his head as Kellan sits down on the bench where Aunt Alice had been. Marcus scans his father searching for anything to be concerned about knowing Kellan would never say if there was.

"So you wanna tell me what happened earlier? Everyone was their normal surly selves then I go to the bathroom to take a leak and when I return it is like I have walked into the twilight zone. Your mother's family actually spoke to me, like a conversation, which they have never done before. Not your grandfather of course but Alice and Rick both asked me about work and other stuff. Maybe they feel bad because of Lauren or something."

Kellan rests his arms on the back of the bench arms spread wide. He flicks Marcus's earlobe with one finger playfully, something Kellan has done Marcus's entire life. The small gesture relaxes Marcus somehow.

"Yeah, maybe so Dad, who knows? They aren't the friendliest bunch of people I have ever been around." Marcus exhales loudly.

"Never have been son, never have been… What are you doing out here?" Kellan asks socially.

"Nothing really. All of this has happened so fast I guess I am just trying to get my mind around it. I don't want to think about it but I can't help but think of Jeff. What is going to happen to him if Lauren dies? Kevin treats him like crap and I hate that." Marcus looks at his father and can see the confirmation of his statement in the now connected eyebrows of his father's face. A frown like that is a sure sign of something profound. It is rare that Kellan is not smiling and joking around. He is a consistently jovial person so when he does become serious those that know him stop to listen, as Marcus found himself doing now.

"Jeff is twelve, older than you were when I got custody of you and Lauren. Jeff is old enough to be able to decide. We will give him the choice and support or enforce whatever decision he makes. Would you be ready to take him if he wanted to live with you? I know you two have a special relationship."

"Hell yes I would! I mean … of course I would take him, gladly."

Kellan smiles at his son. "I would as well. He is a great kid, he deserves to feel loved. All kids do. Cassie is Kevin's daughter, so we can't give her the choice and honestly it isn't like she ever gets treated like anything other than the hanger of the moon, right?" Kellan chuckles softly.

"*Right*!" Marcus laughs too. "Hopefully Lauren will pull through, she is insanely stubborn, if she doesn't want to give up she won't." Marcus reaches over and pats Kellan on his muscular arm, noting the tears in his father's eyes.

"Let's hope son, let's hope." Kellan says softly.

Marcus looks at his father for the first time as though he doesn't know him, appraising what he sees objectively. Marcus can see the lines of age and laughter that crease from the corners of his eyes following the curve of his cheek bone. They are not the deep creases worn by most men his age; they are the thin lines of repetitive pressure on his skin. They are proof of years of smiles and laughter. It is the face of a kind man who enjoys life. Further proof of Kellan's love of life is his somewhat protruding belly. At fifty-four years old, Kellan has a powerful upper body, strong hands and arms, strong thick legs, but Kellan isn't what you would call a fit man. He has always had a thick waist as most Irish men do, but the once thick cords of muscle on his back are no longer strong enough to keep his stomach flat and his pelvic girdle defined from his hips, as they once did.

Kellan considers his Fathers physique in relation to his own, never having noticed before how different their structure is. Their similarities are limited to the same thick strong legs and developed calves, wide square shoulders and the exact same hands. Marcus could now see for the first time in his life his resemblance to his mother's family. Like Luis and his uncles, Marcus has a waist that is dramatically small in comparison to the width of his shoulders; his limbs and torso are proportionately longer than Kellan's. Kellan has the stalky bear like look of his Irish genetics, whereas Luis has the long sinewy but powerful musculature of an Elk. Marcus's joints and bones are much smaller in proportion to his frame than Kellan's bones are to his own stout frame. Marcus looks back and forth between himself and his father, considering that perhaps the small, almost dainty size of his wrists compared to the more block shaped look of his father's is why he looks so much more defined than Kellan.

Rising from the bench without a word, Marcus gives his father's hand one last pat. Looking at the reflection of his own frame and stride in the tinted glass of the automatic doors, Marcus can see that he is the half-way point between his father and his grandfather. He has the width and bulk of musculature passed down by Kellan, but the grace, length and small waist given to him by Luis, via Diane. Marcus had never thought about it before but between the two men he was blessed to have an exceptionally well-proportioned body. Smiling he thinks, I should workout harder; it would be a shame to waste my genetics.

Marcus has always been physically active. He was an athlete in High School and in college. He had been good enough to get a full ride scholarship to play basketball in college but hadn't taken the sport seriously enough to make it a career. Marcus could have tried harder and put in more work to make it to the NBA and had even had one or two interested teams but he couldn't see himself making basketball a job. He would have ended up hating it. Not to mention his height deficiency. He is 6'4" tall. Small for a professional basketball player. Recalling something his father had said to him in high school when he had been taller than most, "You can teach fundamentals and plays but you can't teach tall and fast." Marcus smiles to himself at the memory.

Instead, he got his bachelor's degree and had made it through college without a single injury to haunt him. Marcus considers that a win in and of itself. Marcus always defined his course in life as; the pursuit of finding, not what he wants but avoiding what he doesn't want.

In all honesty Marcus doesn't know what he wants. He only knows that what you want *in* life and what you want *out of* life are two extremely different things. At twenty-six he hasn't decided on either.

Upon returning to the waiting room, Marcus interrupts Lauren's latest Doctor as he was telling everyone to go home for the night. That he expected no change in Laurens condition for at least another twelve hours, allowing time for the antibiotics to take effect.

Marcus gathers his coat and stumbles zombie-like to his truck. Kevin had said Marcus could stay the night at the house with the kids. Kevin was going to stay at the hospital with Lauren so Marcus was in effect doing him a favor by watching the kids. Marcus is happy to do it since he had not had a chance to spend any time with Jeff. Cassie was already at the house with Kevin's mother, but she had to go to work in the morning, so Marcus would bring both kids back to the hospital in the morning. Kevin had said that Jeff was at a friend's house and should be home later in the evening. "Hopefully Cassie doesn't freak out on me. She is too little to remember who I am." Marcus mumbles to himself.

Sliding into his seat Marcus feels the strain of the day seep into his consciousness. He had been too worried about Lauren and too distracted by his animosity towards Luis that he hadn't allowed himself to feel anything. Now he feels tired and sad as well as curious about what his Aunt Alice had told him. He contemplates her advice on the drive home and considers it to be of great value while also realizing his knowledge of Luis and Janie is minimal. He feels self-centered in his lack of knowledge and his past lack of desire to even get to know them. "To be fair, they didn't make much of an effort to get to know me either. They weren't exactly what grandparents are expected to be."

-6-
Jeff

Pulling up in front of Lauren and Kevin's house he can see the light on in the foyer. Marcus is both surprised and a little affronted when Kevin's mother answers the door before he even mounts the steps to the patio. She meets him on the stairs with her bags in hand and tells him where the key is, waddling down the walk to her car without as much as a goodbye.

"Maybe their generation is just rude, or maybe you just get that way when you get that old." Marcus mumbles as he locks the door behind him. To his right Marcus can hear a soft chuckle. Jeff had been sitting on the stairs waiting for him. Marcus strides over and hugs Jeff, lifting the twelve year old off the floor.

"You are squeezing me too tight Uncle Marcus, I can't breathe." Marcus kisses the boy on the forehead and sets him down. Looking at his nephew, love swells in his chest. It is like looking at himself at twelve with the exception of Laurens impossibly thick hair and dark caterpillar thick eyebrows. Marcus hugs him again softly. "Shouldn't you be in bed big man?" Marcus asks Jeff.

"Yeah, like I am supposed to be able to sleep." Jeff scowls down at his feet. Marcus can see the hard set of Jeff's jaw as though the boy is trying not to cry. Jeff's profound sensitivity and intuitive intellect is what Marcus has always loved about him. Jeff is a good hearted and kind kid even though he is smarter, better looking and more popular than most of the other kids his age, he is good to everyone. There isn't a hint of bully in Jeff. He even dotes on Cassie although she is treated much better by Kevin than Jeff is. Marcus smiles, knowing that will probably change as they get older but hoping none the less that Jeff is not ruined by resentment as Lauren had been.

Marcus ruffles the thick spikey hair on Jeff's head. "Hey, no matter what, I am going to be here to take you, or take care of you, whatever you need… ok?" Jeff looks up into Marcus's face, the shining hope in his black eyes making Marcus's throat swell with emotion. "Don't look surprised little dude, I love you. I am here for you. So is Grandpa Kellan. We are family Jeff, we are going to make it through this, and your mom is tough. I know she is going fight, you should know that too. Now, how about we *try* to get some sleep? Want to show me to my room or couch or whatever?"

"Sure Uncle Marcus, thank you." Jeff says meekly.

"Don't thank me yet minion, I will be getting you up first thing in the morning with a whip, driving you like a slave as you fry my bacon, and I won't want there to be any complaining out of you." Marcus says in a poor impression of an Irish brogue. Jeff laughs and shows Marcus to the guest bedroom.

In the morning Marcus waits until Cassie awakens on her own, to get the kids started for the day. She toddles down the hall hugging Sully from Monsters Inc. Marcus recognizes the electric blue monster from the movie he had watched with Kellan just months ago. They had both agreed that the little girl from the movie looked exactly like Lauren had looked when she was a little girl. Cassie is the spitting-image of her mother, as a child, and thusly the little girl from the movie as well. Cassie has the same large deep set eyes as Lauren and Jeff with the same thick eyebrows that make her angelic face seem constantly brooding. Cassie is extremely adorable; Marcus thinks to himself as the knee high little girl looks up at him, craning her neck to Marcus's full height. Cassie freezes in mid step and glowers at Marcus.

"Hello Cassie, you probably don't remember me. I am your Uncle Marcus, your mommy's brother." Cassie continues to eye him as though he is a monster preparing to eat her but trying to lure her with kindness. Tilting her head suspiciously, Cassie scowls wearily at Marcus until Jeff rounds the corner and hugs Marcus. Jeff wraps both of his arms around Marcus's waist, saying, "This is Uncle Marc Cassie, we love him." Cassie's eyebrows lift releasing her eyes from the tight grip of her glare, into a look of serenity.

"My mommy isn't hewe," She states sadly. "She is bewy sick in the Hos-pal." Marcus softens and drops to his knees in front of her, still towering over her slight frame.

"I know baby, I am going to take you there a little bit later to see your Daddy and to see if your mommy is doing any better, okay?" Cassie nods then sidles over to Jeff and wraps herself around his leg, Sully still clutched tightly in her arm. Jeff hugs her to his thigh protectively to comfort her.

Following showers and breakfast the kids get dressed. After wrestling with Cassie's car seat for ten minutes, Marcus loads them into his truck before they head to the Hospital. Cassie is chatting animatedly about something Jeff understands but Marcus does not. It is something to do with a kids TV show that Marcus is unfamiliar with, but he enjoys hearing Cassie sing the theme song in indistinguishable baby syllables. Her voice is so cute it almost tinkles and drastically improves Marcus's mood. By the time they reach the hospital Marcus is humming along and finds himself feeling grateful to God for the innocence of children.

As the three of them extricate themselves from the truck, Marcus walks around to Jeff's side to make sure Cassie doesn't have a problem navigating the height of the truck. Jeff reaches to help Cassie but she pulls away. "I want Unc Mawk get me." She says, making Jeff pull a shocked face.

"Wow, ok." Jeff says to Cassie. Turning to Marcus he says. "It usually takes her a lot longer than that to like someone." Cassie lunges trustingly from the truck seat into Marcus's arms. He catches her neatly and kisses her face as she giggles, then wriggles from his grasp to the ground. Marcus smiles thinking; having kids doesn't seem that bad.
Entering the Hospital together, Cassie locates her father and runs to him. Kevin scoops her up kissing her absently as he nods in conversation with a doctor Marcus had not seen before.

Marcus enters the waiting room, mildly surprised to see that it is empty with the exception of Luis. Marcus had expected the small room to be as full as it had been the day prior, but upon consideration realizes that elderly people feel the strain of sitting for long hours much more acutely than he himself would have. Cataloging his various body parts Marcus acknowledges that he is stiff from the long drive and slightly padded wooden chairs of the waiting room as well. Looking at Luis, Marcus marvels at the old man's erect posture and military bearing, Luis's spine is ram rod straight and he is looking down at something in his hand.

Marcus rises on his tiptoes to try and improve his vantage point but still cannot see what Luis is holding. Marcus wonders to himself why he is so curious until he looks closely at his grandfather's face. There is a look of such tenderness and longing that Marcus feels as though he has walked in on young lovers in their first tryst. It is obviously a deeply intimate and private moment, in which Marcus immediately feels shameful and intrusive. Averting his eyes Marcus attempts to act as though he had not seen Luis. Marcus treads as lightly as he can to the bank of chairs on the opposite side of the room from Luis. Seating himself gingerly on the chair, Marcus immerses himself in the inspection of the fabric pattern on the padded arm rest.

"You must still be angry with me for my remarks about your Father yesterday." The smooth depth of Luis's voice travels easily to Marcus although Luis had said the words so softly.

Looking up, Marcus can see that Luis is still engrossed in the object he holds. Marcus shrugs then realizes Luis will not have seen him. "I was angry yesterday, I am not any longer. I apologize, Grandfather, if you felt disrespected. It wasn't my intention to speak harshly." Marcus says in a formal tone that he himself finds curious. He doesn't know what it is about Luis that makes him speak as though propriety is of the utmost importance but that has always been his grandfather's effect on him.

"Well son, you were correct in part as a grown man to defend your Father and to make your argument plain. I respect you for that. I have also wished in the past that your Father had at least tried to put me in my place, right or wrong. I would have respected him more if he had. Your Father shouldn't have taken that much grief from me, but he earned my disrespect by how he treated your mother and even more how he let her treat him." Luis finished with a stern look of finality that clearly challenges Marcus to argue further. Marcus does not argue further, he only nods his understanding.

"Come sit here boy," Luis pats the chair to his right, "so I don't have to yell at you from across this room." Marcus rises and does as his grandfather bid. Once seated he glances quickly to his left at the object in Luis's hand. It is the care worn photo of his grandmother that Luis had shown him the day before. Marcus retracts his gaze and leans back to look at the ceiling, not knowing if he should say something or what to say if he should. Marcus settles for staring at the cheap plastic florescent light panels above his head.

"Have you ever been in love boy?" Luis asks Marcus in a forlorn tone.

"No, I don't think I have yet." Marcus answers without moving.
"That is just too bad, love is a great and painful and wonderful and horrible and amazing thing. It defines life. It defines us as human beings." Luis says in a tone that transcends longing yet is so profound that Marcus can feel the goose flesh rise on his arms. Marcus shivers as a chill passes down his spine and settles somewhere near his navel. He drops his head to look into the wizened face of the man next to him, somehow now disconnected from him in his knowledge of what Marcus has yet to experience. The man who has loved for life, next to the boy who never has, Marcus finds himself longing to belong to the other man's world, to have that knowledge no matter how great and terrible it may be.

"What is it like to love someone Grandpa? My dad has tried to explain to me how to recognize it when it is happening but not what it is like after it has happened." Luis laughs heartily.

"Yes well, those are two differing things aren't they? I suppose it must be different for everyone so I can only tell you what it was like for me." Luis pats Marcus's knee with his free hand while shaking the photo of Janie in his other. "She moved me. The first time I saw her, although it wasn't the first time she had seen me. She told me some years later that she had noticed me the first day I came to mass but I hadn't seen her until I had been going to that church for a couple months. She always sat in the back between her two parents and I had always sat up front by myself. I had no family I had left them all in Guadalajara so I could come to the United States and make money to help my Family." Luis pauses looking at Marcus in disbelief. "You don't want to hear all this, it is a long story." Marcus moves to the edge of his seat and turns halfway to face Luis.

"I do want to hear it. If you want to tell me, I will listen. Please Grandpa, go on." Marcus looks around the room as his grandfather is doing. They are still alone.

"No one has ever asked me to tell it before. Go get me some water and I will gather my thoughts. I don't want to tell it out of order." Marcus rises to make the trip to the vending machine down the hall; he can hear Luis whispering behind him to the photo. "You hear that darling? I finally get to tell someone about you… my angel." For some reason Marcus's throat feels thick and dry. He rushes to the machine to get several bottles of water, knowing intuitively that he is going to be glad he thought ahead.

Marcus returns to Luis's side, his arms laden with several bottles of water and a cup of coffee for each of them. Luis refuses the proffered coffee as he reaches for a bottle of water. Marcus smiles secretly, grateful to have both steaming cups of the dark liquid to himself. Luis speaks softly between swallows. "Janie drank a pot of coffee a day when we were teaching at Wyoming University. I never drank the stuff, too bitter." Marcus nods his head in understanding.

As the two men settle into their chairs, Luis begins to speak. "I was only seventeen when I came to this country. I barely spoke English as it was my fourth language. I rarely had needed to use it growing up in Central Mexico. I had decided to leave home and come to the United States to get a job, so I could help my parents raise my fourteen brothers and sisters. I was the oldest and considered it my duty and honor to take on the responsibility of my terminally ill father, as the head of the house. My mother was a hard worker and took on laundry from many of the town's people, which brought in just enough money to barely feed us. I had just finished my education or High school as it is called here in America. My mother wouldn't allow me to get a job prior to completing my schooling. Education was of utmost importance to my parents. They believed it was the only way to improve our lot in life. I too believe that as you very well know." Marcus nods at Luis's statement. He does know.

Marcus halts Luis as he is about to continue, "Fourth language, English was your fourth language? What were the other two besides Spanish?"

Luis grins, "Oh, well, my father was full blooded Mescalero Apache and my mother was full blooded Tzapoteca Azteca. So my first languages were Nuhuatl and Apache. Which incidentally is a bastardized version of the Anasazi dialect, as the word Apache is really the Anasazi word for enemy. It was Apacho until the white settlers came and mispronounced it…anyway, a little history lesson for you there. Somewhat off topic. However, when I decided to come to the United States, I decided to completely integrate and didn't speak any other language than English. I learned to love the language and that is why I decided to become an English professor later in life."

Luis resumes the original story, obviously eager to share. "I had only been out of school for three days when I packed up my two pairs of pants and two shirts, kissed my brothers and sisters and left without a peso to my name. I walked from Guadalajara to California in 1937." Luis laughs at his own recollection. "It was a drawn out walk almost fourteen hundred miles. As I traveled, I took small manual labor jobs that paid me mostly in food and any money I did make; I immediately sent to my mother, with the exception of a new pair of boots, I had walked holes in mine. It took me months to reach America. In those days the border was much easier to cross than it is now. I slept in back alleys and storage rooms in the shops that I worked for no more than a week at a time. Every morning I would wake up grateful for a place to wash out my clothes and a place to sleep. I wish now that I had kept a journal or memoir. I was young and determined. I was not the cerebral student of life that I had to become later." Luis pauses, his eyes unfocused, obviously they were looking into the past at a much different time. Marcus waits, finishing his coffee.

Marcus nods appreciatively of his grandfather's conviction. He can't imagine walking fourteen hundred miles for *anything.*

I had traveled towards the coast of the Pacific and had just arrived in California on June 8th. I remember the day exactly because it was the day of a Solar Eclipse. I felt God was sending me some sort of sign that my life was changing and evolving and chose to take that event as a positive sign. I crossed the border into this country in the seven minutes of darkness that the eclipse provided. I felt moved and blessed. It was a beautiful moment for me only second to the day I met my Janie." A single tear follows the deep lattice work of Luis's face getting lost in the laugh lines running from his nose to his chin.

"Wow, a solar eclipse is quite a sign." Marcus says in awe.

A deep chuckle in Luis's throat makes Marcus turn back to his Grandfathers face. "Yes, I felt divinely singular, never considering that perhaps, God could have been sending a sign to many more people in the world than just me." Luis states with sarcasm that Marcus was not aware the man possessed.

"I was young and full of hope for myself and for my family. I didn't think beyond the need to feed my siblings." Luis drinks deeply form the plastic bottle in his hand. With a long sigh the elder man continues. "It didn't take long for me to realize my own foolishness and how far away our one room house in Guadalajara had been from the problems of the rest of the world. Within a month I was aware of so much more than I could have ever dreamed possible. The German Gastapo was already in power and arresting people for religious reasons. Ireland was fighting for a new constitution, Japan was invading China and many more world affairs. I was overwhelmed with the need to become part of the world."

"I had come to America to play baseball. I had thought that was my calling and a means to feed my family. I was hoping to make enough money to bring them here to the United States. I had dreams of riches and grandeur that only an indigent boy from Mexico would think possible. I didn't realize that the color of my skin would make me only eligible to play in the Negro League and that there were so many more talented men trying to make a name for themselves. I had been hoping to play with the Los Angeles Angels in The Pacific League but that was not meant to be. After two years in Missouri playing with the Kansas City Monarchs, I watched from the bench as they won a championship. I decided to go back to California and enlist in the Army where I felt I could be more useful and closer to my family. I had made enough money playing baseball to bring one of my brothers to California from Mexico where he had gotten a job working in the Orchards as a field hand. Between the two of us we had sent our mother enough money that she would be able to bring the rest of the children to California within another six months. My father had just died and I wanted her here so I could take care of her and the rest of the kids. I didn't want to be in Missouri when my mother arrived in the States. So I went back home to California." Luis finished his sentence with a pat on Marcus's knee, indicating a good stopping point.

Marcus looks at his watch. It is almost eleven. The small waiting room is filling with the rest of the family and a couple people who must be family of another patient. "Grandpa, are you hungry? Would you like to go to the cafeteria?" Marcus asks.

"Oh, well sure, I could eat something." Luis says, his previously furrowed brows lifting, surprised that Marcus would ask.

Marcus rises, turning to assist Luis to standing. Luis insists on walking to the cafeteria despite the long trek down the corridor and across the bridge crossing over the street to a separate wing of the Hospital. Marcus does not keep track of the time as he allows his mind to wonder, admitting to himself that he is truly excited to hear the story his grandfather has to tell. Luis is obviously less frail than he looks. As he ambles slowly towards their destination, several hospital staff members ask if they need a wheel chair. Marcus laughs when Luis indignantly says. "I am old, not sick. Isn't there someone around here that is asking for help? This is a hospital after all. Someone has to be looking for them while they are nagging me."

The cafeteria is bright with the morning sunshine and florescent lighting that seems both unnecessary and conflicting to the natural light. Marcus is glad it is morning as he is sure that in the darkness the room would seem as hostile and cold as a State Prison despite the faded prints of beachscapes lining the unevenly coated eggshell walls. Marcus notes that it is comfortingly clean and devoid of patrons this early in the day. "There aren't many people in here grandfather. What can I get you? A sandwich? It shouldn't take long." Marcus looks the short distance to the menu posted above the kitchen counters and the waiting line cooks.

"They probably don't have it, but I would love a pork chop sandwich." Luis says mournfully. The distant expression in his eyes indicates that he is again deep inside his own thoughts. A wistful smile flits across his features, lingering momentarily at the right corner of his still full lips. Marcus scans the black ribbed board with the off kilter white letters.

"Sorry grandpa, No pork chop sandwiches. How about a French dip?"

"Oh sure." Luis says dismissively but without angst.

Settling in to eat their early lunch the two men sit in silence. The food is not bad, better than Marcus had expected. He has never been a fan of the French Dip style sandwich as it has a distinctive lack of crunch that Marcus considers so satisfying in the well toasted sandwiches that he usually orders. He finds himself anxious to eat quickly, so he had ordered what he had ordered for Luis, impatient to get back to his grandfather's story.

Concentrating on their food, the two men do not notice the tall beautiful girl as she walks into the cafeteria. She had noticed them though and was just thinking to herself how they simultaneously didn't look a thing alike as she initially walked in the room, but how as she passes there is something in the symmetry of their faces in profile that are exactly alike. "Hmmm." She mumbles to herself in unrealized vocalization.

The soft sound attracts Marcus's attention. As he looks up, she is just looking away and narrowly missed making eye contact. Marcus's sandwich froze halfway to his open mouth as he watched the stranger float past their table and into the back kitchen behind the serving counter. Marcus tilts his head as she disappears behind the white ceramic tiles of the wall.

"Shut your mouth boy, or you'll catch flies." Luis instructs his grandson. Startled, Marcus nearly drops his sandwich in his lap; fumbling to catch it he saves his pants by funneling the scattered sandwich to his plate. "What's the matter son? Leave the iron on at the house?" Marcus frowns not understanding the reference, as he attempts to reassemble his sandwich. He looks up to see Luis has finished his sandwich. The older man has a look of deep concentration. Marcus imagines this is the expression Luis would wear when perusing a wall containing an interesting selection of novels. Perhaps he is looking through the many volumes in his head, Marcus muses silently.

"Ah, we were discussing my family." Luis says as understanding dawns in Marcus's expectant eyes. He thought I was having a dawning moment earlier when he asked about the iron. Marcus chuckles to himself. "Yes, grandfather, you were at the part where your mother was coming to California with your brothers and sisters."

"Yes, of course, that is what I was just saying. I'm not completely senile yet you know?" Luis chides good naturedly. Marcus bows humbly coaxing a wide grin from his grandfather.

"You know I am a good catholic as was your grandmother?" Marcus nods indignantly, he does indeed know. His grandparents had always been unyieldingly devout, and judgmental of others religious choices. "It hadn't always been that way." Luis continues. "When I had been here those few years without my family I rarely went to church. I rarely had time, but when I returned to California knowing my mother would be here in a matter of months, I decided to return to mass to avoid upsetting her and wanted to be established and known in the church before she got here and found me out." Luis says down his nose as though sharing a naughty secret.

"I found a quaint church that was not a long walk from the house my brother and I lived in. It was just inside the boundaries of a much nicer neighborhood and I know my mother would be happier to worship there than at the mission for all the immigrants. Although I was already a citizen and spoke English so well that no one even guessed I wasn't born in California, my mother barely spoke English at all. She was a proud but kind woman and she has a desire to completely integrate into our new lives. It isn't that she wanted to leave our culture behind, but she did want to leave our way of life behind and make a better life for the rest of my siblings." Luis pauses as Marcus rises to clear their dishes from the table, returning with water and coffee.

"So within two weeks of getting settled in our new house, I began to go to church every Sunday. I made the effort to get to know father James and to make sure he knew me. I warned him of the imminent arrival of my mother and the rest of my family," Luis smiles ruefully, "and father James was enduringly kind and helpful." Marcus smiles back at his grandfather, seeing a hint of his sense of humor, and the love of his family as Luis spoke.

"My brother Manny was not so pleased to be forced back into a pew but he too was terrified of our mother. She was small but fierce and even as grown men we had respect for her wooden tamale spoon." Luis makes a sharp quick chopping motion towards Marcus's hand indicating what would be an impressionable blow delivered by a wooden spoon. Marcus laughs softly nodding his understanding. Picturing his tiny and ancient great grandmother chasing a younger Luis around a kitchen with cooking utensils, he laughs a little harder.

Luis pins Marcus with a stern look in his eyes but a grin on his weathered face. Marcus is deeply enjoying himself.

"Manny *did* enjoy church very much in the end. It was full of pretty young girls that were more than willing to sneak off and whisper sweet secrets with him. Manny was the most handsome of all of us and had a big grin that never left his face. He is the only person I have ever known that could transcend racial barriers with a smile. His huge dimples, perfect teeth and impeccable manners didn't hurt his cause. Manny broke many hearts in our congregation… of all ages." Luis laughs heartily remembering his brother with fondness.

"Mama, was the only woman that was never fooled by his charms and he knew that, so off to church we went. We had been members of that congregation for three or four months before Mama arrived. She arrived late on a Saturday night and unpacked all night, then stayed up until it was light out to iron Sunday clothes for all fifteen of us before going to sleep Sunday morning. I had pressed her to stay at home and rest while I took the kids to church but she adamantly refused. "Luis," she said, "God doesn't take a break from listening to our prayers so I am not going to take a break from thanking him." She had only gotten a couple hours of sleep before we were off to Sunday mass."

Luis begins to stand so Marcus rushes to his side. "Young man, I don't need you to hen peck me. I just have to excuse myself to go to the restroom." Marcus releases Luis's hand and sits back down as he watches Luis cross the room slowly.

-7-
The Lily

Marcus looks around noticing that the cafeteria is now full and bustling with people in a rainbow assortment of scrubs and lab coats. The lunch hour rush must have hit while he was engrossed in Luis's words. Looking at the clock on the wall it is nearly two thirty in the afternoon.

As his gaze drifts lazily from the clock to the bland frames on the walls, he catches a movement from the corner of his eye. It is the young woman he noticed earlier. She has glistening dark hair, so glossy it looks like the sun has embedded in the strands. It hangs loosely down her back in soft waves. It is almost ebony dark but glints purple/red as she walks past a sunlit window. She moves with a swift, powerful grace that reminds him of his girlfriend from college. She must be an athlete, he thinks to himself. Her skin is the most unusual color he has ever seen, as though someone had found a way to blend cinnamon in milk effectively. Her face looks so soft and inviting to him. Not so much, soft in texture, as the texture looks to smooth to be considered soft, but soft in the roundness of her features. The arch of her brow flows into high curve of her cheekbone, across full cheeks to a perfectly round nose that reminds him of a baby, into pouty lips that look almost too full to be real yet are in perfect balance to the rest of her face. She does not have a baby face, she is striking and exotic but so alluringly soft looking, like the arch of an

Asiatic lily. He is mesmerized by the perfection of her profile. She is incredibly beautiful, gorgeous even. Marcus is so engrossed that he does not realize he is staring until the screech of Luis's chair makes him jump. Luis laughs as Marcus nearly topples over in the lightweight chair.

"See something you like son? If you are looking at that raven haired beauty over there then I would say you have impeccable taste." Marcus colors under his cheeks and makes a show of adjusting his chair to the proper position.

"I was staring pretty badly huh?" Marcus asks Luis guiltily as he stares at the table top.

"Yes son, I would say so. You are lucky she didn't catch you. Security would have come and taken you off to the funny farm." Marcus frowns up at his grandfather.

"The term they use now is nut house, grandpa."

"Well whatever it is called now-a-days, you should be ashamed… gawking like that will make a young lady uneasy." Marcus's head snaps up to defend himself and is confronted with an uncharacteristically mischievous grin stretching his grandfather's face. Marcus laughs good-naturedly.

"I suppose so. You want to head back to the waiting room or go outside for a walk?"

"A walk I think. These old bones are creaking from sitting so much. I feel like the tin-man from the Wizard of Oz." Luis says as he begins to toddle in short steps towards the automatic doors that open to a shady courtyard. Marcus catches up to Luis in time to hear. "You know an old man can't really talk too much about staring at the ladies. You could have built a hornet's nest in my mouth the first time I saw your grandmother and it would have gone unnoticed."

Marcus cuts his eyes in Luis's direction, a sly look on his face. "Oh really?" Marcus cajoles as they walk along the sidewalk in the sunshine. The scent of ripe apples and tulips permeates the air in the full heat of the afternoon sun. Marcus inhales deeply, sighing his contentment as he considers how at peace he feels here at Luis's side, joking with him in a way he had never felt comfortable doing before. They have walked three laps around the courtyard before Luis settles on a bench and begins to speak.

"Oh yes, your grandmother was quite a looker as you well know. Her skin seemed to be the smooth perfection of milk in a crystal decanter. She was pure luminescence to me in that baby blue dress with the white lace collar. The first time I saw her was also the first Sunday I took my mother to church. After mass I was standing on the grass in front of the church playing with my youngest brother and sister, surrounded by the other twelve of my siblings, Mama was on the stairs, deep in conversation with Father James when I saw Janie come out of the front doors and float down the stairs. She was arm in arm with her parents but I didn't even see them. All I could see was her perfect face. She was smiling and laughing with her father when she looked up at me. It was like I had been caught in an ice storm. I was instantly frozen solid and the world went silent. Our eyes locked for just a moment but she didn't look away or bat her eye lashes shyly like most girls would have back then. It was a different time and girls were supposed to be shy and coy. Not my Janie. She stared back at me boldly, curiously and it made me instantly aware that she was different than any girl I had ever laid eyes on before." Luis releases a huge sigh. Marcus looks at his grandfather and is shocked by the transformation. Luis looks thirty years younger, as though the memory of his love has erased a large portion of time from his visage. Luis's face seems to glow with the light of that day. Marcus feels that light infuse him with energy as well.

"She was challenging me with her eyes and would not have looked away if her father had not shaken her. She had not heard his question and when he looked at her face he had seen that challenge there too. Following her gaze his mean, hard stare landed on me. It was the worst look anyone had ever given me in my life; worse than all of the bigoted remarks that had been thrown at me from the stands in the baseball games, worse than all of the prejudice people who had thrown me out of their stores when I asked about jobs. Janie's father instantly hated me." Luis grunted in dismay but continued.

"You see, during World War II there was very little difference in races. There was white then everything else. Janie's parents were Black Irish and were intensely proud. They were determined to protect her from the prejudice they had faced when they were back east. In the eastern part of the United States, the Irish were no more well liked than the Chinese or Black people, and they had been mistreated. They did not want Janie to be subjected to that and they didn't want her to be around anyone who would be. She later told me that on that first day, her father had forbid her to even speak to me. Your grandmother being who she was, that only made her want to talk to me more, so I suppose I should have thanked old Ailfrid O'Brien for that." Luis chuckles, Marcus follows suit.

"I had never seen Janie before that day but she had been going to that church since she was a little girl. She knew everyone in the congregation and she was the model Catholic daughter. She was happily involved with the church activities and every member of the congregation adored her. She was Father James's sweetheart. So of course he was the first person I asked about her the following Sunday. He had told me that she and her parents sat in the fifth pew from the back on the left side of the main isle every Sunday. I had always sat in the second row from the front of the church, on the left side, waited until the church emptied, then went home, which is why I never saw her. After that my family started to sit on the right side, no further back from the pulpit as Mama wanted to be as close to Father James as possible, but I wanted to be able to turn and look at Janie so we switched sides. Mama of course never knew that."

"Every Sunday I would catch myself looking for her and if I heard any noise from the back of the church I would always turn and look hoping to see her get up to go to the restroom. I had vowed that I would follow her and talk to her just as soon as I had the chance. Her Father's eagle eye never once missed it when I turned to look. He would stare me down with detest in his eyes. You know the term, "if looks could kill," I would certainly have been dead a thousand times over if Ailfrid had his way. I would always smile at him ignoring the animosity in hopes that he would one day smile back as Janie always did when he wasn't looking."

"Months and months went by and she never got up from her seat. I was starting to lose faith and I was starting to run out of money from baseball and odd jobs. My family was now settled into their new home, schools and Mama had set up her own laundry business so I had decided to enlist in the Army. Father James announced it in church two weeks before I was to leave for Basic training. I still had not gotten to speak to your grandmother, and by then other girls had started to notice not just Manny but me too. There was never any hope for those girls. My heart belonged to Janie even though I had never even spoken to her."

"The next night I went to the church to pray for my family and for God to place me in Janie's heart and not let her marry by the time I came back from Basic." Marcus shifts to look at Luis and can see that his face is still alight with joy and love. The expression on Luis's face alone is enough to humble Marcus. Marcus is in awe of the depth of emotion that his Grandfather still has for his long dead wife. It is like his love and memories of her keep her alive. As long as Luis is alive to love her, she is immortal. It is such a powerful thought that Marcus's eyes become moist with unspent reverence. Marcus can't help but think that he hopes to be immortal in that way or one day for him to keep someone immortal with his love. Although he has never been in love he can recognize the rarity and enormity of love that profound.

"Grandfather, it is windy, let's go in and see what they have to say about Lauren. Ok?"

Luis rises as he pats Marcus on the knee. "Yes, let's go see your sister." He says a forlorn yet happy look crosses his again aged face.

-8-
Unrecognizable

Marcus is no longer thinking of the inevitability of love. After visiting Laurens room and having a long conversation with her doctors, Marcus is more consumed with the inevitability of death.

Lauren is indeed unrecognizable in her current state. She is swollen from head to toe as though she had gained two hundred pounds in forty-eight hours. Kellan had been right; the only part of her entire person that was familiar was the unusual color and thickness of her long blue-black hair. Her face resembled a mound of bread dough that had lashes embedded where eyes should be and stretched, colorless worms where lips should be. Even her pert button nose was no more than a slightly raised bump in the flat roundness of her face. Marcus had nearly broken down wondering if she could possibly ever look the same or if her face and body would resemble a deflated balloon if she were to recover from this.

She had been adorable with her fair skin and the smattering of light tan freckles across her pert nose and high cheek bones. Marcus couldn't get past how unfair it was for this to happen to Lauren and her children. She was a good hearted person, with a quirky sense of humor and a deep devotion to her job and family. She has her issues with Kellan and Diane but she is an all-around good person. It just isn't fair.

Marcus punches an empty hospital bed that is sitting in wait in the long deserted hallway. Glad that the mattress was there to vent his anger on, knowing if it hadn't been, he would have hit something more solid instead. Again, praying inside his head as he makes his way to the waiting room to join the rest of his family. Placing his balled up fists as deeply in the pockets of his jeans as he can, he ambles slowly down the hall, willing his anger to dissipate before facing his Father, knowing it would upset Kellan.

As Marcus nears the waiting room, Kellan posts inside the doorway, waiting for him. Without speaking Kellan and Marcus exchange looks of deep worry for Lauren and concern for each other. Kellan steps forward from the doorframe, extending his arms to his grown son. Marcus circles his Father with his own arms as Kellan clutches him fiercely. Marcus notices for the first time that he is taller than his father now but how comforting it still is to know his father is there, still the pillar of strength and love that he had been when Marcus was a young boy. Marcus is filled with a great affection for his Father and is deeply grateful he is here and that even in his gruff imperfections, he has always succeeded in making Marcus feel loved, supported and protected.

Moving to release Kellan, Marcus waits for Kellan to comply. When Kellan does loosen his grip Marcus still holds his father by the Biceps in a friendly grip, not wanting to let go just yet. "Hey Dad, I just want you to know… you are a really great father and I am really glad you raised me. I am lucky to have such a good man for a father." Kellan drops his head, stifles a sniffle and walks wordlessly to the restroom. Marcus allows him to leave, understanding Kellan's need to recover.

Marcus enters the waiting room, hoping to have a few minutes of his own to recover. Luis waves him over. Marcus approaches slowly, feeling beaten down and tired.

"So you want to take me for another walk? I already went to the restroom so you won't have to see to that…" Luis entreats with a mock scowl. Marcus feels his face lift in an unwilling smile. "I will tell you, the worst thing about being an old man is everyone wanting to treat you like a pet. Everyone is always trying to feed me and make me pee when I don't need to." Luis glares at Aunt Alice. She makes a dismissive motion in his direction like he is a feather to be waved away. Marcus smiles in spite of his sadness, suspecting that was Luis's goal.

"Sure Grandpa, I can use some air." Marcus follows Luis out of the waiting room and down the long hall towards the cafeteria courtyard.

Passing through the hiss of the automatic doors, Marcus notices the clear sky that had earlier been a bright cornflower blue is now a much darker Lapis. The lights around the courtyard are flickering in their attempts to illuminate the darkening path. The foliage seems so much more private and close to them now as they walk around the patch of grass surrounding the fountain centered in the courtyard.

Marcus doesn't have anything to say and is rather hoping Luis will break the comfortable silence before he has too when Luis starts talking. "I suppose there is something I should say to comfort you about Laurens condition." Luis rubs the white and grey stubble that is barely evident on his chin. "I just don't know if anything I say would be a lie in the end and we are both grown men. Suffice to say… I hope she recovers, as do you I am certain." Marcus makes a noise halfway between a sigh and a grunt. He still cannot formulate anything to say, his mind and heart are too heavy for words. He pats Luis on his stooped shoulder, allowing a few more minutes to pass.

"So where were we?" Luis asks rhetorically. "Ah, I was going to the church." Luis smacks his lips as though stretching them for a workout, Marcus looks up.

"Are you thirsty? I can go get a bottle of water."

Luis smiles graciously. "No, no, I am fine, maybe later."

Luis sits on a bench, Marcus follows, sitting beside Luis with his legs extended, ankles crossed, hands interlocked on the back of his head, settling in to listen.

"I walked into the candlelit church, smelling the polish someone had used to clean the wooden pews and the slightly burnt smell of wax. It was a scent that made me feel comforted and protected. A sense of calm and rightness filled me. I somehow knew I was doing exactly the right thing, being there in the church at that moment."

"I walked to the kneeling benches in front of the prayer candles and began to pray. I prayed with all my heart for the safety of my family in my absence, my own safety and confessed my love to God in whispers. I thought I was being quiet, feeling as though I needed to say it all out loud, as though it somehow gave my words more solidarity. I told God that my heart had always belonged to him first and my family second but now I found myself torn with the need to give my love to another. That I felt as though I would not have lived a complete life if I never had a chance with Janie. Confessing openly that I felt my true appreciation for God and life in general lived within her." Marcus's eyes widen as he stares at the sky, wondering how that must feel. Imagining how conflicted it could make a man to have to walk away from someone who had such a strong pull.

"I must have knelt there in front of the Virgin Mary for hours. When I got up I felt stiff and weary in my body but light and hopeful in my heart, truly believing that God would help me realize my path."

"As I brushed off my pants and rearranged my clothes I got a strange uneasy feeling, as though I were being watched. "Hello?" I said to see if anyone was there. No one answered but I thought I heard the rustle of fabric. I waited but heard nothing else. I took my hat out of my pocket and started for the door, my footsteps echoing on the wood floor. As the doors closed behind me, I put my hat on my head, staring up at the stained glass windows above the portcullis, admiring the old world style of the architecture. It began to rain, so I turned to leave. By the time I took three steps it was pouring buckets. Just as I got to the end of the walk the doors of the church burst open and Janie ran out into the rain."

"Lew-ees? Right?" She had asked. Shocked that she knew my name and equally shocked to see her alone I looked around for her father or his car, thinking he was going to get out and shoot me. I ran to her, grabbed her hand and pulled her back to the portcullis, out of the rain.

Her emerald green dress was getting soaked and looked like it weighed a lot, the skirt full and billowing with lots of fabric, her black hair falling in ringlets, stuck to her face, the coif loosened by the torrents of rain. "What are you crazy?" I asked her. I don't think I had intended to say that, I just said whatever came to mind. I was stunned silent thinking she would be angry but she just laughed, it was the most beautiful sound. I had never heard her laugh and it tinkled in the acoustics of the narrow space."

"Yes, I think I am." She said, the excitement and fear making her eyes glint in the darkness. "I think I must be, my father would kill me if he saw me here soaked through in the rain, alone, with you. He will be here any minute to pick me up you know?" I looked around, a bit nervous myself, when I noticed that I still held her hand. I wanted to let go but I couldn't, she was so warm and alive just as I had seen her in my dreams."

Marcus was enthralled, excited for the young man he pictured in his mind. "What was she doing there?" He asked Luis.

"Well, she was there doing what I was doing, she was praying." Luis laughed. "She told me later she was there to pray for me. That was many years later, I won't skip ahead." Luis pats Marcus's knee.

"Standing there holding her hand, looking into her beautiful eyes, her lashes thick with drops of water, I took out my hand kerchief and patted her face dry, marveling in the joy I felt just looking at her. Knowing right then that I was already in love with her. Happy beyond measure that her pulse was throbbing in her throat, she was nervous, but she didn't drop her gaze as any other girl would do. She stared up at me, into my eyes, at every feature on my face, as though seeing another human being for the first time. She said to me so softly, "You are so beautiful" and reached up and touched my bottom lip with her fingers, tracing them ever so gently. I was completely amazed at how the happiness coursed through my veins. Like wild fire. I would have kissed her right then. I still think I should have, but car lights flashed around the corner and we jumped, hiding in the dark corner in case it was her father. It was, he pulled up to the curb and opened an umbrella to meet her at the steps. "Tomorrow night. Here!" She said and ran out into the rain to meet her father so he wouldn't find her with me."

"I tell you boy, there had never been a better moment in my life up to that day. My heart had wings, I felt lighter. I felt infinite, like I was suddenly part of the energy of every other living thing in the world. I swear to you I didn't even feel the rain. Dazed with happiness I half skipped and half strolled through the rain back to my house where my mother fussed at me until I took a bath and went to bed. Can you believe she stood outside of the bathroom ranting at me about catching my death? She was always so stern, no matter how grown up I was." Luis smiles fondly at the memory of his tiny, admonishing mother. Marcus smiles as well, wishing Diane could be remembered so fondly.

"Every day after that, I thought about her all day long at work and would rush home to eat before I went to her. Every night, for the next two weeks, we would meet at the church. We would pray and then we would hold hands and talk. She told me about her parents and their history. They were first generation Irish immigrants that had lived in Boston until Janie was born, but had decided to move west to avoid the hatred of the Irish that was so prevalent in the East. Her father and mother both had come from old world money and he now owned a grocery store. He was a hard worker and considered all Hispanics to be hardworking but dirty field hands that were beneath his notice, although, he bought most of his fruits and vegetables from those "Dirt diggers." This made me think how amazing it was that Janie did not share his opinions as most young girls were servile to their parents in those days. On Sundays, Janie and I would make darting eye contact but never spoke to each other or acknowledged each other to our families."

"During our meetings, we shared everything with each other. I told her that I was Aztec and Apache, and how I had grown up in a one room shack in Guadalajara with all my family. She was astounded by the fact that I came from such a large family and wished she had brothers and sisters. She told me about college, playing basketball, only half-court at the time, how she has always been fascinated with how things work and especially airplanes. She was so fascinating and strong minded compared to other women. Her father's relations in Ireland were well-known moguls who owned the Irish Times newspaper. She explained how her father had married her mother Eva, who had been direly poor but extremely beautiful and was completely docile and subservient to her father. I think that is why Janie was so head-strong. She didn't want to be like her mother. She was a rebel, she wanted her own life and I wanted to give it to her." Luis smiles sadly but with so much energy that Marcus smiles with hope as well.

"She was certain that her father would learn to respect me and my family for our fortitude and strong faith. I told her as the weeks passed about my journey from Mexico to California. I confessed all of my hopes and dreams to her and even how I thought God had sent that eclipse just for me. She said. "I think he must have done, Luis, it was a sign that you were coming to me, because I felt that same thing when I watched that eclipse, and I know it was telling me you were on your way." I remember sitting holding both her hands, facing her on a bench much like this one." Luis indicates the bench he and Marcus are seated on.

"All too soon it was only two days until I left. I wanted her to know how I felt, I didn't want to leave without telling her and I knew that was the moment. "Janie," I said, "I am about to leave for Basic training in two days and I will be gone for a couple months." I had never done it before but I grabbed her and hugged her to my chest, hard, wanting to feel her heart beat next to mine. She hugged me back, just as tightly, so I whispered into her fragrant hair, smelling her clean scent for the first time. "Will you wait for me? Please say you will and when I come back a respectable soldier, I will *make* your father see. I promise." She pulled away from me, tears in her eyes. "Yes, I will, I will wait for you."

"I was so happy I wanted to jump, sing, and dance like a fool in King Arthurs Court. I would have if her father's voice, calling for her, hadn't interrupted us. Janie got up, kissed me on the forehead and ran back into the church to meet her father. Ailfrid was a terrifying man. More because I was scared he would punish her than being scared of anything he could do to me. I actually wished he could like me because I felt so grateful to him and his wife for having created Janie. Part of me loved them both for giving her life, but part of me hated them for stifling her gregarious and independent nature."

"I walked home singing Do Nothing till You Hear from Me, By Duke Ellington. It was 1944, I was twenty-five, in love and floating down the street." Luis stands up, stretching his lower back gently, a little off balance. Marcus stands up next to him, just in case, but doesn't reach to assist him, remembering how proud Luis is. Luis begins his slow totter, back down the path and Marcus follows alongside him. Marcus's eyes rise to the night sky noticing how brilliant the stars look tonight, twinkling with mirth just as the glint in his grandfather's eyes, as he tells his story.

Luis continues as though he had not taken a break. "When I got home, I was caught under a wave of curious family. I had not spoken to anyone about my feelings for Janie. I had not wanted anyone's candor or criticism. The one thing about having a large family is the lack of privacy and solitude a person needs in those moments. I would have safely made it onto the bus to Basic Training without so much as one suspicious word from them if I had only remembered that Janie had been wearing red lipstick." Luis chuckles. "I was floating on cloud nine and it never crossed my mind to look in a mirror before joining my family for dinner. When my mother accosted me in the kitchen with a deluge of questions about my dalliances, I was so confused. Thinking maybe someone had seen Janie and me at the church or maybe my mother was suddenly a mind reader. Something I had wondered often throughout my childhood." He laughs again, running his hand over his mostly bald head.

Marcus thinks of the many good hearted but firm natured mothers he had seen in movies and sitcoms and imagines his great grandmother as one of them.

Luis pats Marcus's hand, before grasping the back of it firmly. "I wish you had had a mother like mine. I don't know where we went wrong with Diane, but you were right yesterday. She wasn't and isn't a good mother." Marcus pats Luis's hand with his free hand.

"Who is the mind reader now?" Marcus laughs. "We all choose to be what we want to be Grandpa. Mom chose not to be there for us. That is no one's fault except Diane's." Marcus states unemotionally. He had come to that conclusion years ago and that had made him even angrier when his mother's family mistreated Kellan, but there was no need to rehash that now.

Luis nods his agreement, a look of admiring appraisal on his face as he gives Marcus a sweeping glance, head to toe. "You sure are right about that son, you sure are." Luis releases Marcus's hand. "Anyway, let's go inside and sit down. I can tell you more once I rest my bones a bit."

Marcus follows Luis back down the long hall to the deserted waiting room. A nurse walks by and Marcus rushes to catch her before she rounds the corner. "Excuse me; do you know where everyone went?" He asks motioning towards the waiting room. The middle aged blonde looks at her watch, slides up the arm of her garish pink scrubs to look at her watch. "Well, it is dinner time, maybe they went across the street for dinner. The cafeteria is closed." She shrugs as if to say, 'that is my guess,' and waddles around the corner and out of sight. A sharp image of the girl he had seen earlier crosses his mind in an instant when the nurse mentions the cafeteria.

Marcus looks at his watch. It is seven in the evening; the day had flown by listening to his grandfather. He removes his cell phone from his pocket and realizes it has been on silent all day, he has several messages waiting. Listening intently for a few minutes he hangs up and asks Luis, "Do you want to go get dinner across the street grandpa? Everyone is already over there, even Kevin and the kids."

Luis shrugs with his palms up, waving his head back and forth in indecision, making the gesture a quirky little dance. Marcus chuckles. "Come on, my treat, you can even have ice cream if you want. Lauren isn't around to nag you about your diabetes." Luis's eyes light up at the mention of sweets, a mischievous air to his jaunty step as he makes his way out the door towards the exit.

Marcus catches up, "If you go into some sort of sugar shock at least we are across the street from the hospital and you won't have to make the drive to the hotel to sleep… right?" Marcus says then cringes wishing he had thought the joke through, not knowing if Luis would understand his wry sense of humor. Luis looks up and glares hatefully at Marcus. Marcus freezes in mid-step, discomfited.

Luis breaks into a wide grin. "If it kills me then I get to sleep in the morgue tonight… also heartily convenient, eh whelp?"

Marcus's shoulders drop as he relaxes into laughter. "It isn't really going to kill you though right?" Marcus asks innocently as they wait for the street light to indicate the time to walk.

Luis shrugs, "Let's hope not." He says then winks at his grandson.

-9-
Worry

Luis made it through an entire Chocolate sundae without incident, much to everyone's relief. Marcus and Luis had made it just in time to order their food with the rest of the family. The meal passed with a tense joviality. It was obvious that everyone was avoiding the topic of Laurens health. The doctors had come and informed the family that there had been no change while Marcus and Luis were in the courtyard. The primary doctor recommended that the family go home and return the next day. The doctors of the Infectious Diseases ward had been working on Lauren's blood work all day and had come up with a unique concoction of antibiotics and detoxifiers that they feel positive will work, but there will be no change expected until later tomorrow morning.

Marcus had not lost all faith in the Doctors but did feel better that they had called in specialists from other departments and experts from other practices. There is something to be said for a Doctor that can admit they are no longer qualified enough to treat a patient. In Marcus's experience, most Doctors had such large egos that they couldn't admit when a patients illness surpasses their knowledge set.

At several points throughout the day he half expected to walk by Lauren's room and see the doctors bleeding her like she is Henry the Eighth. Luckily for everyone he had not witness any such atrocity.

Marcus has a kind face but a build that emanated strength and power. Many professional people found him to be terribly imposing and intimidating. Marcus always thought that was odd and amusing, as they had no idea how far they would have to push him to raise his ire. Although, admittedly, Lauren's failing health does have him on the edge of flipping out on anyone who showed the slightest ineptitude. Mostly he knows that he is just looking for a reason to vent his feelings on someone. Nearly seventy-two hours and Marcus still feels angry and helpless. It is the longest he has ever been under such a high level of emotional strain in his life.

Marcus runs his fingers over his head, through his hair, down his neck, settling on his trapezius muscles to rub out some of his own tension. His muscles are rock hard as though he is flexing and he makes a conscious effort to try and relax them. It is useless.

Luis walks next to him without a word. Marcus wonders how he can feel so exhausted when his eighty-two year old grandfather is still hanging on with no signs of weariness. Marcus lets loose with a great groaning sigh. Luis looks up into his face. "Don't grieve for something you haven't yet lost son. It will help no one feel better and only make you feel even worse, then guilty when it turns out to be unnecessary." Marcus nods at the wisdom in that statement, but thinks, that is easier said than done.

Let's go sit for a while then you can drive me to Alice's hotel... peppermint?" Luis offers the red and white candy to Marcus. Marcus accepts wishing it was a lemon drop instead. Lemon drops had been Luis's big treat for him when he had been a small boy. Luis would slip him lemon drops all day on the few fishing trips they had gone on together.

Luis leads the way back out to the courtyard, clutching the water bottle he seems to always have present. The weather is perfectly cool, with a slow, lazy breeze to rustle the apple trees the smallest bit. If Marcus were alone he would find a park, a blanket, a place to lie down in the grass, and then look at the stars he rarely got to see clearly in Las Vegas. As is, he settles in next to Luis's frail form on what he now thinks of as "Their Bench."

Marcus reminds Luis, "You had just gotten home from the church when grandma had promised to wait."

Luis rolls the peppermint wrapper around and around his index finger as he collects his thoughts.

"Ah, yes, the red lipstick." Luis begins with a deep breath.

-10-
Red

"My mother was talking so fast about philandering and confession and how I had lied about being at the church that it took me a moment to understand what had set her going." Luis chuckles. "You see? Mama thought I had lied about going to church and had been off running around with some cheap floozies." Marcus coughed at the old fashioned term.

"My little sister Anna had stood behind Mama, pointing at my forehead then her own, then at the mirror. I got the hint and looked in the mirror in the entry way. There, dead center, on my forehead was a perfect setoff lips, puckered and creased in an obvious kiss. I thought it was lovely. I would have gotten it tattooed there if I thought my mother wouldn't carve it off and send me to basic training without a face. Which I am sure she would have. Instead I took out my hanky and placed it over Janie's kiss, rubbing the back of the cloth to transfer the kiss, folded it up and put her kiss in my pocket. I kept that kerchief with me everywhere I went. I never laundered it. I was scared the kiss would be washed away." Marcus shakes his head in amazement, impressed with his grandfather's devotion at such a young age and in such a short time.

"There are many annoying things but also wonderful things about having a large family. That night I was interrogated by every single one of my siblings after my mother had gotten finished with me. I had stayed as tight lipped as I could; only telling them that I had met a girl and that she was special. I did not tell them who she was or that she went to the church we went to. On Sundays, Janie and I would make darting eye contact but never spoke to each other or acknowledged each other to our families but after that kiss, my mother would have had her eyes peeled. It wouldn't have been long before we were found out."

"The night before I left for Basic Training we met at the Church again. I had brought her a single rose and a promise ring. It had been a ring my grandmother had worn and my father had given it to my mother. My mother had given it to me the day I left for California."

When I got to the church she was already there waiting for me in the little courtyard we always sat in. She had said she had trouble getting out of the house. That her father had wanted her to stay home and spend some family time but her mother had intervened and told Janie to be gone only an hour. We only had a few minutes left before she had to walk home. I had planned to walk her at least to her block. We were sitting on our bench holding hands when I let go to retrieve the ring from my pocket. I was just putting it on her finger when Ailfrid had screamed at us. Janie began to entreat her father to understand to beg him to listen. He was in a rage and when he walked forward I stood up and put myself between them. He was screaming at her, sweating and dangerous looking, telling her she was a harlot and how she was a waste of all his effort. Janie was crying. I had said "Mr. O'Brien Sir, I mean no disrespect but you are not going to talk to Janie like that. She is a good girl. We haven't done anything wrong sir. We haven't even kissed. I wouldn't do that. I wouldn't do anything to compromise her… I love her."

"Ailfrid told me he was going to kill me and that he would talk to his daughter however he damn well pleased. But I wouldn't let her go, I was holding her between my arms behind me. I told him. "Sir, you are going to have to kill me if you think I am going to let you hurt her."

Just then, Father James showed up, with his robes flying. He had heard the commotion and thought someone was robbing the church. He tried to talk to Ailfrid, to calm him down. He told me, "Son, you should let Janie go."

Janie clung to me, holding me in a tight hug from behind. "No, Father James, I don't want to go." She held tight to my hand as Father James pulled her away from me with the hand still holding tight to the rose I had given her. She eventually let go, crying and begging. I felt so helpless, until she ran back and kissed my cheek.

Ailfrid went insane. He grabbed her around the waist and was carrying her to the door when he set her down and ripped the ring from her finger, crushing the rose. He threw the ring at me. It hit me in my chest and fell to the ground. I felt like he had stabbed me in the chest. Now she wouldn't have anything to remember me by when I was gone. "She will never be with the likes of you." Ailfrid said to me and dragged Janie screaming and crying into the church." Marcus is unaware of the anguish in his own eyes until the crease on his forehead began to throb, straightening his features, he continues to listen.

"I yelled after them. "She will! She will be with me. I will come back for her. I will find her." Then I stood frozen until I heard the squeal of his tires from the front of the church. Father James tried to comfort me. He said a great many things to me that I didn't hear. I just grew hard hearted and determined. I knew I would never rest until I was with her. I vowed to myself and to Father James that I would be with her when I came back from Basic Training. I would make Ailfrid see sense." Luis stretches and reaches for his bottle of water, taking a long drink as though to collect his thoughts.

"Grandpa, why do you think Ailfrid hated you so much, had you two ever had a run in?" Marcus asks trying to understand the passion of a man that would drag his daughter away in tears.

Luis's eyebrows raise high in consideration of the question. "No, until that day, we had never spoken to each other. Not once, not even in passing." Luis sets his bottle down and rubs his face with both hands as though trying to scrub away some dirt. "I think he was just scared as father's sometimes get, wanting the best for their children."

"Janie told me years later that Ailfrid and Eva had wanted a large family but that Eva couldn't have any more children. Janie had three infant siblings that died at birth or late in her mother's pregnancy. Ailfrid and Eva were extremely over protective and domineering. They had poured all of themselves into Janie and her education. They felt as though she deserved to marry a doctor or lawyer. They wanted her to be with someone who was in the same financial class as they were. They felt she was too good for me and I confess, I agreed with them. But unlike them, I knew that I would be lucky to be with her, but did not believe she would be unlucky to be with me. I knew how much I loved her and that I would die trying to give her the world. I went home that night with a heavy heart but also knowing that my honorable intentions were valuable. I also knew that Janie wanted to be with me too and that was enough to sustain me." Luis inhales and exhales loudly, almost a groan.

"Are you tired Grandpa? Would you like me to take you to the hotel now?"

"Yes, I am tired, but not the way you think. I am tired of living my life without her. These last four years without her have been the loneliest of my life. I can't wait to be with her again." Luis says, lifting his hands to the heavens as though silently pleading for God to grant his wish. Closing his fists and shaking them angrily before they fall down to his lap. "Let's go to the hotel now. We can go get a drink. I think I could use a stiff orange juice. How about you?" Marcus laughs.

"Sure grandpa, I could use an orange juice too, as long as it has some Tequila in it."

Luis shoots Marcus a shocked glance. "A boy after my own heart." Luis pats Marcus on the shoulder as they exit the Hospital grounds. The two men walk to Marcus's truck in silence. No sooner does Marcus hear the click of his seatbelt then Luis starts back in on his tale.

"The next morning I got up early. I had thought all night about what happened at the church and didn't get much sleep. My mother hadn't asked me why I put her ring on a chain around my neck. I had intended to keep it there close to my heart until I saw Janie again and I would give it to her then. As luck would have it, I had to give the necklace back to my mother before I got on the bus to leave. After my induction into the Army where I said my oath, the Drill Sargent's recommended that we leave all valuables with our family. So I left the ring with Mama but I kept my kerchief with Janie's kiss."

"I was inducted at Ft. MacArthur, a few miles from Los Angeles, then sent to Camp Roberts for 17 weeks of Basic Infantry training. I wasn't allowed to visit my family on the weekends or to leave post at all. I think it is much the same in Basic Training now. No weekend leave passes." Marcus nods in agreement as they wait at a stoplight. Knowing several of his friends that had gone into the Army and were not allowed any leave until after they were placed in their vocational training or at their permanent duty station, after Basic.

"Basic Training was a lot of fun for me. I was learning so much and so fast that I didn't have much time to dwell on my plan for Janie. My anger with her father was a great motivator though. I excelled quickly, becoming a squad leader then a platoon leader within the first month. I loved being a soldier. I loved feeling like I was part of something much bigger than myself. I was proud to be a citizen of the United States and I considered it a privilege to have the chance to fight for my family and Country."

"Although I missed Janie and thought of her every second; I was learning something new, I was happy and optimistic. Life felt wide open for me. Every night I would say my prayers with Janie's kiss held close to my heart. Then I would tuck it under my pillow, promising her from my bunk that I was going to marry her and take her with me, wherever I got stationed as soon as I got out of training. Those 16 weeks flew by and I was confident that Janie would be waiting for me, just one week left until graduation."

"I remember it was a Monday when we went down to mail call. I was expecting something from Mama of course. She always sent me encouragement, scriptures and cookies or cinnamon rolls. When my name was called I got my care package from home and a letter from Father James. It was the only letter he had ever sent and I thought it was weird that he would wait until my last week. I thought maybe he was welcoming me home. He wasn't. His letter was short and to the point. It said;

"*Luis,*
*   I am sorry to have to be the one to tell you, but I thought someone should and I didn't know if there was anyone else who knew about you.*
*   Janie and her family have moved away. They sold the store and left a few days after you left.*
*   After praying on this for some time, my conscience told me to tell you. I am sorry. I wish I could help but I have no information about where they went. I didn't want you to come home with the expectation of seeing her.*
*   I hope you can forgive me for being the bearer of bad news and your mother for giving me the address where you*

are. Remember, if God wills it you will find her and you will be together.

Have faith,
Father James.
P.S. She loves you."

"I read that letter at least a thousand times in my life. Eventually I ripped off the last three lines and kept them folded inside the hanky with Janie's kiss. I needed to keep the affirmation of her love with me to keep me strong. I thought about writing to her but had no address, her old or her new. So instead I just held her love in my pocket and touched it every chance I got." Luis chuckles as they sit in a quiet corner of the lounge in the hotel. "I got in trouble with my superiors constantly, for having my hands in my pockets, but it was worth it. To me that hanky was like a tether holding me to the earth. As long as I had it my soul would not float away, without it I would be lost."

As Luis pauses, Marcus considers how little he has said in the last two days. He isn't sure if he had ever listened to someone so intently in his life. "You know grandpa, this is such a good story that I think I have been the most quiet I ever have. How come you have never told it before?"

"Well, because no one has ever asked me too. I am just an old man after all. What do old men have other than old news?" Luis shrugs dismissively. "People, especially young people are too embroiled in their own lives to take the time to hear about someone else's."

"That is just sad grandpa." Marcus frowns. "Unfortunately, I think I am usually one of those people, just going about my business from day to day, not wanting to be bothered by the lives of other people. I always felt I was just minding my own business, but listening to you I realize; there is a difference between caring enough to be curious about others and being nosy. There are interesting people out there. Like you." Marcus finishes his water and sets it next to his empty juice tumbler.

Luis smiles and shrugs again, an almost disjointed looking motion. "I am glad to tell it, our story. It makes me remember things I haven't remembered in ages; the look of her creamy skin, dripping with rain water, the scent of her hair that first time, even how she seems to never have aged from that day in my mind." Lifting his glass to his grandson he says. "So thank you for that son."

Marcus feels humbled, folding his hands on the table in front of him, almost shyly he responds. "Sure, you are welcome I guess… anytime."

Marcus looks around the modern but modestly decorated lounge. It is one of those places where anyone could be comfortable. You could show up in jeans and a T-shirt to have shots with friends, or you could be having an after dinner drink with a date or business acquaintances. The large room is just dark enough, with tables far enough apart to imply privacy, yet warm and rich in espresso and gold. The table candles and wall sconces allowing enough light to be inviting and comfortable as opposed to seedy and hidden, as many hotel lounges tend to be.

Marcus leans back in the booth propping his extended arms up on the top of the back rest. Arching his back and stretching he asks, "Are you ready for bed yet? I am kind of worn out. It has been a long day. I could sit and listen to you all night, it is cathartic but I don't want to keep you if you want to get some sleep."

Luis considers the question with narrowed eyes, "I think I could get some sleep. You can come pick me up in the morning and we will have breakfast with Alice before we go to the hospital. Would that work out for you?"

"Absolutely Grandpa, I would love to. How does eight o'clock sound?" Luis nods agreement. "Great, I will walk you to your room then." Marcus leaves money on the table as they leave.

-11-
Beginning

Another bright morning greets Marcus as he is shaken awake by Cassie. Her face is only scant millimeters from his when he opens his eyes, causing him to jump in alarm. Cassie giggles her precious little laugh. "You wakey up Unk Mawk? Daddy say the hosp call and time to eat." Marcus sits up, taking a moment to make sure he isn't naked. He can't remember getting into bed last night and hopes he didn't fall into habit and completely undress for bed. Lifting his sheet and blanket to peek he is relieved to see he has on boxer briefs and basketball shorts. Feeling a small warm hand on his arm he tucks the blankets around his waist, still uncertain what is appropriate in front of Cassie. Looking at the tiny hand caressing his arm his gaze follows her limb up to her face. She is looking at his arm with curiosity.

"Something the matter Cass?" Marcus asks. She just frowns so he rephrases. "Are you okay? Is my arm okay?" Marcus holds still, not sure what she is doing. Cassie frowns deeper, and then her eyebrows shoot apart into a precocious smile.

"Yes, arm okay, just bewy big Unc Mawk," She says matter-of-factly then frowns again at the spot her hand is still settled on. "No haiw der eve-a?" It takes Marcus a moment to understand. Oh, he thinks, "No hair there either," He says aloud.

"Nope, no hair." She enunciates as she rubs his arm a little more, and then removes her hand to chew her finger. "Not like daddy, him haiwy." She wrinkles her little nose, looking just like her mother.

Marcus's heart flips over by her cuteness but is saddened by the resemblance. He looks at the clock it is nearly seven. Jumping out of bed he is about to shake off his shorts then points out the door. "Out you get rug rat." He smiles and winks at Cassie, she giggles with both hands on her lips and runs out. Slipping on his jeans and a sweatshirt, he admonishes himself for sleeping late and not showering but knows he will miss Luis if he doesn't hurry. "Aw well, I can shower tonight." He mumbles as he glides from the room to the top of the stairs.

"That is exactly what I was thinking." Jeff says teasingly as he follows Marcus down the stairs. Marcus pauses at the foot and whispers to Jeff. "Hey you want to ride with me to go get Grandpa or you want to go with your Dad?" Marcus shakes his head in the direction of the kitchen.

"Oh, no worries Uncle Marcus, I am going down the street to work on some homework with friends. Mandy's mom will drop me at the hospital after." Knowing what Marcus was getting at, he leans in conspiratorially. "I am ok, I promise." Marcus nods then lifts Jeff into a bear hug, carrying him into the kitchen with his arms pinned at his sides. Jeff wiggles ineffectively. Marcus does not release him.

"So Kevin, I promised the old man I would have breakfast with him and Alice, you didn't make anything for me did you?" Jeff grunts in his attempts to loosen his uncle's grip. Kevin looks up and frowns at the affectionate display.

"If by anything you mean, did I make you any pop tarts? Uh… no, I figured you could manage." A gruff smile crossing his lips as Cassie attaches to Marcus's leg.

"Le-go, Le-go my brudder, you skeez to hawd." Marcus laughs and sets Jeff on his feet.

"Thanks Cass." Jeff says with his hand on his chest as though he were just finally able to breathe.

Marcus picks up Cassie and kisses her swiftly and sets her back down before heading out the door. Yelling over his shoulder as he leaves, "Call me if you need me to pick anything up. See you at the hospital."

Speeding down the highway Marcus digs in his toiletries bag on the seat, locating his toothbrush, brushing his teeth on the way to the Hotel. He arrives in the front lobby at exactly eight, glad to be on time.

Entering the lobby, Marcus spots Luis waiting in a chair reading a newspaper. Alice is across from him knitting something unidentifiable, a large ball of variegated yarn, in alternating hues of crimson, espresso and caramel at her side.

Alice and Luis lift their heads in unison as Marcus approaches. Alice is the first to speak, greeting Marcus as she stands opening her arms inviting a hug. "Good morning good lookin', if you aren't the picture of Daddy when he was your age, I don't know who is."

This statement takes Marcus by surprise. He had never considered his facial resemblance to Luis before. Marcus looks in a mirror mounted on the wall just above an ornate table and inspects his face as Luis slowly rises. Remembering the black and white picture Diane had showed him of Luis and Janie when he was a child. He can't remember much detail but he can see the same chiseled lines of Luis cheekbones and full lips in his own face. Looking at Luis now he wonders if this is what he will look like in his eighties. Marcus shrugs, thinking; if that is the case, I could do worse for genetics. "Thanks Aunt Alice, I will take that as a compliment." Luis guffaws good-naturedly.

Marcus turns to follow Luis and Alice into the dining room located on the far left side of the Hotel Lobby. Much like the Bar on the adjacent side that they had been seated in the night before, the décor is classy, and simple with clean lines and comfortable seating. Unlike the bar the colors are somewhat brighter and less private. The booths are upholstered in thick distressed burgundy leather with the nail head buttons down the side, but somehow lacking in the old world Midwest theme that most studded furniture proclaims. The lines of the room and furniture are more modern and sophisticated, no rolling arms or ornate balustrades as Marcus had expected. The muted tones of chocolate, khaki and rich mauve make the room feel warm and welcoming.

Marcus watches Alice unceremoniously shove the ball of yarn into her oversize carry-all, he asks. "Aunt Alice, are you making something to match this room or did my eyes deceive me?"

Alice looks around as though seeing the room for the first time. Laughing she says, "It certainly would seem that way wouldn't it? Although I don't think any of these chairs need a sweater." Marcus chuckles as they all settle in to wait for the waiter.

Breakfast is enjoyable, the food is good quality and prepared to perfection. It feels good to have a belly full of warm hearty food after five days of barely eating. Since Kevin's call, Marcus hasn't felt much like eating and had begun to feel weak and somewhat depressed. This being the first, full meal he has consumed since then he acknowledges that lack of food has a definite effect on his mood and makes a note to force himself to eat even when he doesn't feel like it.

"Well, that was good, I feel much better now, don't you?" Luis asks.

"Marcus, you look ten shades better honey. You were looking awfully pale the last few days. A big boy like you, you have to feed those muscles. It won't do your sister any good at all if you die of starvation. You need to keep up your strength for the kids." Alice says patting Marcus on the thigh.

"That is a point well-made and was exactly what I was thinking. I will try to do better." Marcus pats Alice's withered hand affectionately. It is so odd to feel this bonded to these people; people he has hardly known his entire life. Family is family I guess, you can't get away from it, and we are all part of each other in some way. Marcus muses inside his head then shrugs.

Insisting on paying the check, Alice scoots from the booth gathering her frumpy ankle length dress around her knees. It looks as though she is being swallowed up by a frothing, foaming, pink, chiffon wave until she stands shaking the mass of fabric out around her, letting it settle like dandelion seeds on a pond. Luis is busy folding his white embossed handkerchief into a perfect pocket square and slides it into the hip pocket of his slacks as he wobbles to standing on his stilt thin legs. Marcus's heart swells with affection for these two elderly people and their quirks, glad to have this short time to get to know them.

Alice walks with a surprisingly strong and lengthy stride for a woman her age, propelling her quickly towards her sedan as Marcus helps Luis climb up into the cab of the truck. Marcus had received a few texts from Kevin during breakfast with a list of errands. Marcus agrees to take Luis with him, so Alice could meet them at the hospital upon their return.

-12-
Hope

Luis sits quietly brushing the wrinkles from his pressed slacks with a look of wonder as he watches Marcus fidget on his phone; jotting down directions on an envelope to the many places Kevin need them to go.

Marcus sighs in resignation as he looks into his grandfather's face. "Well, it looks like we have our hands full today. You are going to be stuck with me for a couple more hours. I hope you don't mind." Marcus winks at Luis as he turns the keys in the ignition. Luis smiles and shrugs in answer.

Marcus pulls out of the hotel parking lot into slow traffic as Luis asks, "So where were we? I may as well finish the story now that we are going to be a while." Marcus frowns thinking momentarily.

"You had just gotten the letter from Father James."

"Oh yes, that's right. Well son, this is the boring part for you and was the hard part for me." Luis clears his throat, placing his hands on his knees and shrugs, obviously working himself up mentally to continue.

"So Janie and her family were gone. I couldn't find them or any trace of them when I returned home from Basic training. I searched, believe you, me. I searched high and low asking everyone in the congregation that I had ever seen Ailfrid speaking to. No one knew anything and if they did they weren't going to tell me. The time came when I had to leave. There was still a war going on and I had promised to do my part. Love couldn't get between me and Uncle Sam. No sir, I said I would go where the Army told me too and so I did." Luis slaps his knee firmly to accentuate his point.

"A month later I was in infantry training and then that spring I was shipped off to Italy where we lost many good men at the Rapido River crossing in the fourth battle of Monte Cassino. We were shipped all over the continent after that. We had just heard news of the fall of Rome to the Allies and I thought of Janie. I always thought of her, but Rome was the home of our faith and the Catholic Church."

"Not long after I was in Normandy when I ran into my friend Joe Smidt. Joe Smidt and I had been in Basic training together. Joe was from New York City and we never left each other's side until Joe got wounded breaking through the Atlantic Wall and was sent home. Joe continued to write to me though and I promised to visit him in New York as soon as I could." Marcus listened intently, forming the maps in his head, remembering these historic records from History classes in college.

In April of that next year I was in The Battle of Okinawa, it was Operation Iceberg and I was in a trench with fifteen other guys I barely knew, we hadn't eaten for days and had been forced back into that trench for the third time and thank God we were, because as I was running for my life and dove head first into that trench my face slid to a stop right in front of my handkerchief; the one with Janie's kiss on it. I must have lost it, dropped it in haste the last time I had been in that trench. If I had not been forced back there, it would have been lost forever. I picked it out of the mud, surprisingly unsullied, still mostly white it was the symbol of all that was good in the world for me. It was hope and innocence. It was my future, my memories and the only piece of home I had left. I lost the bit of letter inside it, but I still had the hankie." Luis sighs, his eyes moist with unspent emotion. Marcus realized he had been holding his breath and releases his own gust of unspent breath.

Marcus tilts his head in shock as Luis erupts in loud cackle of laughter. "You know, three days later an air force regiment dropped food down over our location. We had to dodge sniper fire to get it but I will tell you, after going so long without anything more than dew and rainwater… Well, it is the reason cold pork chop sandwiches and a Hershey's bar still fill me with the happiness and contentment that a gourmet meal would for most other folks. When you are starving a full heart cannot replace a full belly and while most of what I dreamt about was Janie… most of what I thought about when I was awake, was how great a saltine cracker would be. Those sandwiches were the best thing I had ever tasted." Luis shakes himself as he twists his finger in the air, as though pulling his prior topic off of a bulletin board only he can see.

Marcus remembers their first sandwich together in the cafeteria and understands the look Luis had on his face when he asked about the pork chop sandwiches. He shakes his head in amazement at the life his grandfather has led and the things he has learned to value.

"In those moments I can only tell you that I became more resolved than ever to find her. I knew that God or some unseen force had led me back from hell each time to remind me of what I had to live for. In the midst of the filth of human denigration and the evil that drives desperate men's souls I had relocated the beauty in my own heart and for me, that beauty had only one name. I knew that Janie and I were meant to be and that I was never going to love another woman." Marcus walked slowly beside the older man, hands laden with shopping bags and dry cleaning, in bewildered silence, waiting for Luis to finish. "As you know, as history will tell you, the war was over by December of that year."

"When I got back to the states, I was on a mission. It seems now, like I had been cold and wet for years before I got to see my mother's face. Truly it had only been just over a year and a half. I went home for a couple weeks to see my family then headed to New York to see Joe. Truly I didn't know why I went to the other side of the country when all I could think about was finding Janie. But I had grown frustrated in California because I just couldn't find any new information. Joe had mentioned taking me to see all the sights in New York and I welcomed the distraction. Something in my soul told me it was what I needed to do. I thought I would find peace of mind there." Luis helped Marcus unload the groceries and other items Kevin had requested, into the back seat of Marcus's truck, then allowing Marcus to help him up into the cab.

"Grandfather, didn't you ever think that *maybe* you were going to New York to *maybe* meet another girl? Didn't you ever doubt grandma's love for you? I mean, couldn't she have met someone else and been married by that time? After all, it had been two years. Two years is a long time, people move on." Marcus inquired gently.

Luis chuckled, "You don't know…" he said playfully. "Two years seems like a lot to you because you are young. I am old now and those two years seem like the blink of an eye… and no, to answer your question. I never thought she was lost to me. In my youth and arrogance I was certain she could never love another. Don't you see son, I *needed* to believe. After all

I had been through and all the ugliness I had seen in war, I *needed* to believe in the seed of hope." Luis gripped his fist tightly between them, holding it up, face furrowed, indicating his determination to cling to his seed.

"Did the two years seem long at the time grandfather?" Marcus asks.

"I suppose they may have if I had not been distracted trying to stay alive." Luis laughs loudly. "As it turns out, war did indeed keep me from focusing on my loss and from being heart sore. Although, I feel confident saying that it wouldn't be so for most men. Most men don't feel the loss before war as I did. They feel that loss when they walk away from their families. They are distracted *by* their pain not *from* it." Marcus looks at his grandfather noticing the faraway look in his eyes, knowing he must be remembering horrors that cannot be unseen.

"When I finally made it to New York it was a grand time for me. To realize the opulence that was available to common men here in America that I could never have dreamed of in my family's one room shack in Guadalajara was awe inspiring. Joe could not stop talking about the shows with all the fancy costumes and jewels that dripped from the heads of beautiful women." Luis pauses to wink at Marcus. "The Ziegfeld Girls were the big thing back then. Janie's grandmother had been a Ziegfeld girl the first time the show opened. But in my time it was the Ziegfeld Follies that people flocked to see."

 Joe took me to tea houses and ale houses where the patrons stood on the long ornately carved bars to recite poetry or bawdy jokes. It was a time of happiness towards the end of the war. So many men and boys returning home to their wives, mothers and daughters. It was a poor country but it was lively in a way that can only be felt. It was infectious and contagious and I was drunk with intuition. I knew that being there in New York was going to change my life and I was impatient to discover how."

Marcus hands Luis a bottle of water and waits, watching as the weathered face emanates a pent up energy, his eyes flashing brilliantly in the unremarkable light around him. Luis finishes half the bottle and sets it balanced on his knee as though it were a dainty tea cup and he a gentleman in waiting.

"Joe and I had been all over New York that week. Every time we left the house I felt a sense of anticipation. I practically skipped everywhere we went and my eyes flitted to every tall dark haired girl I saw. None of them were my Janie of course. I thought I had seen her in Grand Central Station once. I never saw the girl's face, just the cut of her shoulders and the sway of her walk in a prim black skirt suit trimmed in white. It is a strange thing to realize how much you love someone by later finding out how much you unintentionally memorize about them. I didn't know I knew her walk like I knew my own face until that moment. I was up on the stairs looking down over the throngs of people making their way to work or wherever they were headed. I raced down the stairs but lost her in the crowd. Two days later I had myself convinced that I was crazy and had imagined it."

"I was due to leave New York and my vacation in two days. Joe had been trying to get tickets to the Ziegfeld Follies through friends of friends." Luis shrugs and looks down his strong nose at his grandson. "You know how well that goes.

Everyone is willing to be your connection until you need a connection as I am certain you must know as a college man?"

Marcus laughs, nodding concurrence. "Yes I do. Every frat boy knows somebody who knows somebody."

Luis raises an eyebrow knowingly. "Yes son, as do all G.I.'s."

"Joe never was able to attain the tickets, which suited me just fine. I wasn't genuinely concerned about seeing the show. There was only one girl for me so no other woman held any charm."

"That all changed as we were walking down Broadway into Times Square. It was August 14th, V-J Day or what you may know as the Day President Harry S. Truman announced the end of the war on Japan. Everyone was jumping and shouting their joy and all I could think of was my Janie. I was wondering what she was doing in that elated and historic moment when I looked up at an enormous sign on a building that said BOND in letters taller than I was. It felt fateful that I was feeling that bond to Janie throughout my whole soul. I was moved to tears boy. I don't mind telling you. I dropped my head to retrieve my hanky, yes, my Janie's hanky and as my eyes followed the line of the building I noticed a poster for the Ziegfeld Follies. I couldn't believe my eyes. I thought I *had* to be mistaken. I began to push and shove through the crowd."

"It was no easy task with all those celebrating people and I wasn't polite about it. I may very well have gotten a blackened eye if people hadn't been in such a raucous mood. I just had to get to that poster and I might have fought God himself if he had tried to stand in my way." Luis sniffles then clears his throat, as he runs his hands over his nearly glass shiny pate.

"When I finally made it to the poster I was astonished. Being bumped and jostled like a buoy in a storm, all I could do was stare at it. It was Janie, taller, more beautiful and statuesque than I remembered. Some of the baby softness of youth had begun to leave her face and a stunning woman was emerging from beneath that incredibly ornate headdress."

"I whooped and hollered like everyone else that day but for a much different reason. I had found her. I grabbed Joe and did my best to shake him to death or suffocate him, as he would surly tell you if he were still alive. He sure told everyone else through the years how he almost had me committed for bolting through the New York crowd without him, only to physically assault him when he found me." Luis chuckles heartily, the vestiges of a younger man breaking through the road map of his face as though his aged skin held a hopeful boy imprisoned inside.

Marcus sees a flashing hint of the handsome youth his grandfather had been. Picturing that younger man so vividly in his mind, he mentally replaces the famous photo of an ardently zealous sailor kissing the girl in all white on V-J Day in Times Square and in his thoughts he can see that couple as his grandparents.

Marcus wraps one arm over Luis's shoulder hugging him gently. "You know Grandfather; I think I would give just about anything to feel that much love for someone. As it is, I think the only people I care even a fraction that much for are Lauren and Jeff, and of course my Father. It just isn't that kind of love. You know I have never been in love, with anyone? Ever!"

Luis guffaws in disbelief. "Never son?" Marcus moves his head in the negative.

Luis inquires further. "Not even a crush in Junior High or High School?" Marcus again shakes his head. "You don't like other boys do you son?" Luis cuts his gaze towards Marcus through the side of his eye. Marcus realizes this is his grandfather's attempt to be comedic and snickers to be conciliatory. Luis plays at a false glare, "its ok if you are funny boy, we will still love you, and we are family. I just won't tell anyone else we claim you." Luis pats Marcus's knees as Marcus erupts in true laughter, his memories taking him back to the man who fed him grandpa surprise.

Luis waits momentarily as the laughter subsides. "As you were son, I am just getting to the good part."

Marcus's grin widens as he gains control, affecting a stony façade making a dramatic show of settling himself to appease Luis. Luis nods his approval, not unkindly, a slight smirk playing at the edges of the deep laugh lines framing his still full lips.

"Please grandfather, continue… pardon my interruption." Marcus says formally, with a sweeping motion of his hand indicating Luis should proceed.

"Let's go see how your sister is, and then I will finish my beginning. Agreed?" Marcus nods as he rises to follow the tottering older man towards the hospital entrance.

-13-
Failure

The Hospital waiting room is empty. There is no one in sight. Marcus had expected to see Kellan or at least Alice waiting.

Marcus helps Luis settle into one of the haggard chairs before setting off in search of anyone who can tell him anything.

After winding his way through a series of hallways he is beginning to feel a bit lost when finds himself in the cafeteria. Marcus is surprised that his first thought upon entering the sunlit room, is of the mysterious girl he had noticed the day before. He searches the room for her to no avail. There are a few stragglers, young and old in hospital gowns with their nearly catatonic visitors but none of them are the girl he wanted to see. Unconsciously letting his shoulders drop, Marcus stuffs his hands into his pockets and shuffles from the room like a dejected child; momentarily forgetting his purpose. He is several steps out of the door when he catches his reflection in a window. He is shocked to see the drop of his posture and shakes himself as he realizes why he had been disappointed. "Huh!" Marcus puffs aloud.

Still inside his head he does not hear his name being called as he meanders slowly down the long hall. "Maarrccuss..." Alice calls. Shouting him down aggressively since she had not gotten a response. "MARCUS!"

Marcus's head snaps up to see his great Aunt motioning for him to come quickly. "Marcus you have to hurry. The doctors have said Laurens kidneys are failing and they don't believe she will last more than a few hours son, I am sorry." Marcus leaps into a full run, his long legs closing the space more quickly than he thought possible. Not cognizant that he has silent tears running down his face until he passes beneath a vent, awareness breaking to cold wetness on his cheeks. He swipes them away as he slows to Alice's side. She leads him to Laurens room.

Lauren is no longer in the smaller ICU room she had been in the night before. It is in a larger room with large machines connected to his sister's swollen body. Marcus cannot comprehend what these machines are doing. It looks like they are removing her blood. Marcus looks up to Kellan's ravaged face, his eyes have sunken in and he looks like he has aged many years since the night before. Jeff is there and rushes into Marcus's arms. Wrapping him in a desperate grip tighter than any boy his age should be capable of. Marcus's waist feels constricted corset tight but he doesn't mind. He pats Jeff lovingly on the head, the question unasked still in his eyes, directed at Kellan. Marcus's eyes shift to the machine then back to his father, his eye brows arch high then into two dark alcoves above his eyes.

Kellan knows his son well. "They put her on dialysis to help her kidneys not work so hard. The massive amounts of antibiotics are killing her organs. We knew that was a danger. The doctors warned us yesterday, remember?" Marcus nods in agreement.

Marcus scans each worried face in the semi-darkness of the hospital suite. He knows that each one of them are feeling what he is feeling; sick to the core of his being at the loss this will mean for everyone. As Marcus considers the impact of Laurens life and death on each person in the room his eyes land lastly on Kevin. After listening to Luis explain the depths that a man will go through for the woman he loves, but had not yet shared a life with, he can only imagine how devastating it must be for Kevin to lose his wife and the mother of his children. Marcus can see the agony and hopeless slump of Kevin's shoulders and feels his own eyes tighten and his throat constrict. In the shadow of Kevin's pain, Marcus feels unworthy of his own.

Marcus finds himself breathless as the picture of the lovely girl from the cafeteria surfaces in his mind.

-14-
Tears

It is three in the morning and the entire family has spent a sleepless night as Lauren hit the peaks and valleys of near death. Marcus is exhausted from the emotional strain of every white coat that walks through the waiting room door making his blood pressure skyrocket in fear. Marcus has never felt more like he was riding a roller coaster or had his ears pop so many times in one night without actually having been on one.

Getting up Uncle Rick says, "I can't possibly sit still for one more second. I can't take this, I have to do *something*." Dragging his hands over his scalp more than rubbing it Marcus can see the middle aged man on his face for the first time. Deep wrinkles, reminiscent of a Shar-Pei puppy, furrow above his eyebrows as his hands push the dual caterpillars into his eyes. Abnormally, ageless with his smooth olive complexion and wise bottomless eyes, Rick usually looks twenty years younger than he is. Now in this moment he looks every bit of his late fifties and then some.

Marcus rises as well. "Me too. I need to move around before I find someone to hit." Marcus gestured for Rick to precede him into the hallway leading to the cafeteria. They walk in silence as there is just nothing left to say. Everyone knows that all the family can do is hope and pray, pray and hope. Then pray some more.

Marcus is doubtful the cafeteria will be open and functional at this hour but he doesn't truly care or need anything. He decides coffee and sustenance couldn't hurt. Looking about he can see small signs of burgeoning employee readiness. There are condiments out on the tables and fresh tomatoes set out to be cut.

"Someone must be here; they must have just gotten here," Marcus states as Rick yawns, nodding his ascent. "You want to just wait and see who shows up? Might be our lucky day." Rick nods again, another yawn beginning, making Marcus need to yawn as well.

Standing at the counter bleary eyed and weary with emotional strain Marcus blinks repeatedly trying to focus on the plastic letters assembled on the menu board as he recovers from his half-yawn. Dropping his head to rub his eyes with the backs of his fist, he hears a silky female voice.

"Are you opposed to owning eyelashes?"

Marcus opens his eyes scowling in the general direction of the pleasantly deep female voice. Whoever owns this voice had to be incredibly sultry and beautiful if she looked anything like she sounded but he couldn't see her. His eyes had begun to water as his knuckles had worried them so harshly. As often happens with tired eyes, the harder he tried to clear them, the more they watered. Tears were now streaming down his face. Not that his eyes hadn't wanted to cry, they certainly had, since Aunt Alice had called him back to Laurens room. So now, for reasons other than what his emotions demanded, his eyes were releasing the pent up torrent.

The owner of the voice misinterpreted his unfortunate malady as true tears and began to stutter uncomfortably, "Uh, oh God, I am so sorry, I didn't mean…" Patting Marcus's back to comfort him, "I just thought you could use a laugh, I thought you were tired. I didn't mean to interrupt, I am so sorry…" The female voice empathizes uncomfortably, obviously distressed at what she considered a grave overstep. Marcus couldn't see but his nose was working incredibly well. She smelled incredible; like vanilla, cream, something spicy and heady, and slightly of … lemons. She smelled like something to eat and now he was beginning to feel uncomfortable himself.

Rick watches his nephew's dilemma with amusement. "Don't feel bad honey, he is tired, he isn't crying. If he were, I would have put him out of his misery already, although you happen to have helped me truly enjoy his angst." The girl immediately releases Marcus feeling suddenly like a weird stranger interloping. Her hands tethered in her skirt as she apologized.

"Well, I am glad my odd groping of a complete stranger can amuse you so." She says gesturing around aimlessly. "I am the staff administrator. I was just coming to check on the kitchen staff."

Rick smiles with evil intent to embarrass and shoves Marcus. "Oh, don't apologize, your groping makes it his lucky day, he was just saying that is what he hoped for."

The girl frowns in distrust. "I am sorry? I was trying to make small talk. I know you all have been here multiple days. Is it the older gentleman that he was with yesterday?" She gestures towards Marcus awkwardly as Ricky hands Marcus a napkin from atop the stainless steel counter top. "Is everything ok?"

Both men answer in unison. "No, he is fine." Rick coughs and covers his smile with his hand. Pausing momentarily to allow Marcus to speak but continues when Marcus does not. "It is *my* niece and *his* sister, Lauren. She has an infection and we could lose her any minute, we have been up all night, we came for coffee or anything really." Marcus had been recovering his faculties with his back to them, and finally turned around.

His mouth falls open unnoticed by the other two people. He snaps it shut audibly but they don't seem to notice. He crosses his arms, then uncrosses them, puts his hands in his pockets, then takes them out, turns left then right looking around for anyone or anything so he doesn't stare at the girl. Ricky notices the motion and turns to frown at Marcus. Marcus freezes.

The conversation halts, Ricky says, "This soggy fellow is my nephew Marcus and I am Ricky, nice to meet you." Marcus shoots daggers from his reddened eyes at his Uncle. Rick shrugs and shakes the girl's hand. Marcus looks at their hands as they meet. Her hands are thin and long but strong and capable looking, both feminine and down to earth with her short naturally manicured finger nails, shiny with a clear polish that enhanced the deep cinnamon color of her skin framing the bright pink flush under the nail bed. Marcus had never seen hands so elegant. Shaking his head he makes a mental note of the fact that he doesn't think he has ever noticed *anyone's* hands ever in his life. A quizzical expression crosses his amused face as he looks up to the girl, *his girl*, from earlier in the cafeteria.

In his haze one clarifying thought surfaces. *She noticed me when I was with Grandpa and she remembers me.* Satisfaction and a new kind of hope clear the remaining fog from Marcus's brain.

Forgetting how awful he must look and the embarrassment he felt seconds before he releases her hand slowly, making eye contact with her he feels as though the world were warping and he is entering some gap in time. Her eyes seem to mist over with pure joy as she stares back at him. His heart seems to come to a complete stop only to accelerate as though leaping from a starting line. Clearing his throat as their hands drop he can still feel the heat of her palm and somehow the texture of her entire personality in the slight but smooth callouses, of her well groomed but obviously hard working hand.

Many things register at once within his mind. This is the hand of a woman who; isn't scared to get dirty, isn't unaccustomed to some sort of labor, isn't scared of anything about herself, is self-assured enough to stare him down and yet humble and kind enough to feel compassion for someone she thought was in pain. This is the firm handshake of a good, kind and un-frivolous girl. She is exquisite but has no idea and isn't overly concerned. She is toned and obviously active, and has an undiscernibly small amount of make-up on if any and she doesn't need it.

Marcus likes her, from within a deep and innocent part of himself, he just genuinely likes her as a person. He *knows* all of that at once right now without any true knowledge of her, yet it is more than a felling, he *knows*. Marcus smiles with an electric excitement of his own as she drops her stare for the tiniest moment of shyness and turns to Rick.

"It is nice to meet you both as well. I hope Lauren recovers. If I can do anything for you while you are here, please don't hesitate to contact me." She hands over her business card to both Rick and Marcus. She turns and disappears behind a door at the rear of the cafeteria behind the counter that reads "Employees only."

Marcus looks down at the card only then realizing she hadn't given them her name; Isadora E. Trevino.

Ricky looks at her card as well. "Trevino; that is a name of Spanish origin, interesting," He gently hits Marcus in the shoulder to get his attention, "and quite a looker." Marcus frowns at Rick. "What? Gay men are better at recognizing beauty better than most kid. That girl is gorgeous and fiery… and she seemed to like you." Marcus's frown turns still darker. "What's the matter? You liked her too; don't even try to say you didn't. I don't know you overly well but you never seemed like a mute moron to me before, not until you looked in that girls face." Marcus scoffs and shrugs but something inside him is buzzing like a busy bee hive.

As the plain girl behind the counter raises doe eyes to Marcus and takes their order he mentally shakes himself

Marcus remembers where he is what he is doing there and feels slightly inappropriate but determined. "Maybe this is my chance." He says to himself, forgetting that Rick was still there.

"What's that?" Rick asks.

"Oh, nothing," Marcus again motions for Rick to exit before him. "I was just thinking out loud." Rick shrugs and takes their tray of coffee and muffins off the counter and out the door.

-15-
Exhaustion

"Lauren is improving. She is finally responding to the antibiotics and they seem to be acting aggressively with the infection. For now we are hopeful and feel encouraged that the cocktail we have come up with is taking a positive course. The dialysis helped remove a lot of toxins and debris from her blood, somewhat clearing the path for the antibiotics… if you will." Everyone in the room listens raptly to Dr. Mashhad as she finishes her update with them.

Marcus feels leery to trust or hope but also feels as though a great weight of impending disaster is averted for now. They have actual reason to hope other than just figurative faith to run with.

Luis approaches Marcus carefully as though he does not trust his legs to hold up his body. Taking Marcus's arm for support the older man leans gently on Marcus and he pats the forearm Marcus has offered. "How about you take this old man to the Hotel so I can get some rest?"

Marcus looks first to Kevin but Kevin has Cassie slung over his shoulder as she snores gently. He waves Marcus off with his other hand indicating Marcus should fill Luis's request. "I am just going to take the kids home and get them in bed. Are you sure you are ok to drive after taking Grandpa back?"

"I honestly don't know. I will have to see how I feel when we get there. I may just get a room and sleep until I am no longer a danger to anyone." Luis pats Marcus a little more firmly this time.

"You can stay on my extra bed. I have two in the room and only take up a small corner of one of them. I am not as robust as I once was after all." Everyone chuckles.

"Ok, it is settled. Kevin, you go ahead and I will take Grandpa back to the Hotel. Alice are you ok to drive, you can ride with us." Marcus inquires with his Aunt.

"Oh, I am just fine it is only four or five miles. If I don't make it, it wasn't meant to be. I am old, I have lived a good life." She winks at Luis who chortles.

Kevin whispers, "And we're off." Turning to walk out.

Marcus once again helps Luis up into the truck. "You know kiddo, I don't remember trucks being this big, and perhaps I am getting smaller."

Marcus smiles, "I know how you feel right now. I feel smaller than I did yesterday." Marcus secures the door firmly and walks around to the driver seat.

The ride is short but difficult for Marcus to remain focused. So much has happened in the last few days. His head is swimming with exhaustion, hope, possibility, happiness at connecting with his estranged family and curiosity about Isadora.

As Marcus gets Luis tucked in he feels as spent as the eighty year old in front of him looks. He feels withered, "Like a flower in the frost." He mumbles as he falls asleep looking at the clock on the nightstand. It is nine in the morning.

Opening his eyes Marcus feels Luis shaking him awake. "Look son, I would love to watch you sleep your life away but I have better things to do. The hospital called. They said Lauren is awake. I thought you might like to know."

Marcus catches the whole speech but it takes a moment to process where he is and what the sentences truly meant. Also that it is dark outside. Looking around groggily he notices the time. It is almost ten… at night. He had slept for almost thirteen hours. "Wow, I guess I was more tired than I thought."

"You think so do ya?" Luis chides, smiling knowingly.

Marcus gets up slowly, feeling his muscles unclench from between the stiff wrinkles of his clothing. He hasn't felt this wrecked since actually waking up hung over on the roof of a house across from the dorms he had been partying in the night before. Stretching and groaning listening to the random popping of his joints he is amused by the expression on his grandfather's face. "Boy you look and sound like you have been to war… well, I guess we went through one last night…" Luis claps his dry rough hands together loudly, startling Marcus. "Anyhow son, that's that. We are out of the proverbial woods now I suppose. Let's go get some breakfast." Marcus laughs and winces as his muscles protest and his tongue sticks to the roof of his mouth.

"How about we stop and buy me a toothbrush first?" Luis agrees a little too quickly for Marcus to not feel a little disgusting.

Entering the elevator Marcus asks, "Grandpa, do they serve breakfast at this hour?"

Luis grins, "They will if they know what's good for them."

After Marcus makes a short detour to the lobby gift shop and the restroom to brush his teeth, they are on their way to the hotel café.

With the food laid out in front of them and little room on the table left, the two men chat comfortably until they are sated. Marcus had gotten a call from Kevin saying that while Lauren is awake she isn't truly lucid and the doctors have asked for the family to wait until morning to visit.

Marcus and Luis find themselves wide awake at midnight with nothing to do.

"Grandpa, do you think you want to finish telling me about you and grandma?"

Luis inhales slowly before responding. "Like I said, I was whooping and hollering and choking my friend to death. Right there in time square with all that joy around me I was certain I was the happiest man alive." Marcus balks at Luis's ability to stay chronologically in place. Shaking his head he settles in to listen yet again.

"For the first time in over two years I saw her. I was so drunk with the sight of her face. I ripped that poster out of that glass case and rolled it up. I told Joe he better get those tickets now. Whatever it took I was going to see the Ziegfeld follies show. If I had to get a job as a stage hand to do it." Luis pounded a determined fist into the palm of his other hand.

"It turns out that Joe didn't get the tickets. He tried as hard as he could even attempted to bribe the ticket sellers at the counter. I ended up using all of my leave. I only had thirty-three days of which I had already used twenty-six when I saw that poster. I had to threaten to go AWOL to get my vacation extended the remaining seven days. The war had ended but my enlistment had not."

"My mother thought I was crazy and was praying for me and lighting candles at the church every night. I had called Father James and he told me how worried she was. I felt bad and thought about writing to my mother and explaining everything to her but I never sat still long enough to get that letter written.

I was half crazed in truth. Every morning that I woke up seemed like another day closer to the end of my life if I didn't find Janie but also the beginning of the rest of my life if I did. That is a tight rope to walk, let me tell you." Luis wipes his forehead as though the memories brought back the physical strain of the time and the sweat that accompanied it.

"With only three days left I resorted to waiting all day long outside of the theater hoping to see her. I asked every person I saw if they knew her. I think it was the second day when they called the police. I refused to leave so they arrested me." Marcus looked wide eyed at his grandfather as Luis began to laugh. He was really getting into the story now. The excitement level was infectious for Marcus.

"Joe had to come down to the station and bail me out. God love him and his silken tongue. He ended up telling the officers in the station my whole story about Janie and my search for her and the little ladies that were the secretaries and file managers talked the sergeant on duty into letting me out Scott free. I was quite lucky and Joe never failed to remind me of how he had saved my backside." Luis laughs good-naturedly again, his eyes far away in the past. "Joe sure was a good friend. I miss that man."

Marcus nods, wishing he could have met Joe, he seemed like a warm hearted character, the way Luis described him.

"Anyway, after I got out of the slammer, I went straight back over to the theater and guess who I see?" Luis slides his palms together in a conspiring manner. "I saw grumpy old Ailfrid. That old goat never looked so good to me. You see… until I saw his face there was a part of me that didn't truly believe that was Janie in the poster. Seeing him made it reality. I was so excited I whooped then jumped back around the corner of the building. I don't know if he saw me from down the alley where he was parked at the back entrance. He came out of the building ten or so minutes later with a raven haired beauty in a red dress with huge fabric roses and one to match in her hair. I couldn't see her face but I knew that it was Janie.

I was so conflicted. I wanted to run up to her that second and steal her away. I wanted to go punch Ailfrid in the face and get in the driver seat of that car. I wanted a million things at once and as I formulated a plan of action they drove away, out the other end of the alley. I ran after them as fast as I could. Just as they rounded the corner I saw Janie look out the back window and spin around in the seat. She had done a double take and my heart soared. I was certain she had recognized me. As scruffy as I knew I was."

Luis wiggles in his chair as though dancing a seated jig. "I ran all the way back to Joe's house, vowing to return to the theater at the same time the next day." Luis drank some water and paused to look out the window into the dark early morning sky. "New York had not been beautiful to me until that night. Everything was a marvel. The ornate buildings and the crush of many cultured peoples, the noise and bustle of the city itself seemed to match the rhythm and energy within me. The cacophony in my head a much louder din than the screeching and honking of thousands of cars echoing off the faces of the structures boxing them in. I was alight in my heart and soul, every woe I had experienced was now erased with the promise within her face." Luis is pacing slowly but excitedly from window to door in the small hotel room. Marcus swallows audibly, almost a frog like croak.

"So was she there the next night?" Marcus asks breathlessly after drinking an entire bottle of water in one tilt.

"No, she wasn't. I arrived at the same time and waited by that same side door. Only an hour or so passed before I got agitated. I nagged the stage hands as they came and went. I tried the box office. I was turned away at every inquiry. I was beginning to go a little mad, I don't mind admitting. I felt like I was reaching down a crevasse for the key to life and it was just out of my reach. I could feel the key with my fingertips but couldn't grasp it. Desperation, I think is what you could call that. I was desperate."

"Finally I found a tiny crank window, stacked up some crates and climbed into the building. It was my last night before I left and I had to do anything I could… Hey, don't look at me like that son." Marcus was frowning in disbelief that his deeply honorable grandfather would break and enter. "I wasn't a criminal I was in love. One day you may well do just as much for that same reason." Marcus conceded with a nod.

"So there I was, dirty and torn and sneaking around in the shadows of back stage trying to find anything I could. All day and night I looked and waited and slunk around and I never found her. The show went on and the building emptied and I was lost. I was defeated. Janie never showed up to perform." Shaking his head sadly without looking at Marcus, Luis sniffed.

A knock interrupts their silence. The hotel maid service had left fresh towels in the hall for them. It is six in the morning.

Luis and Marcus agree to try and sleep for a few hours before returning to the hospital.

-16-
Relief

Marcus jumps from the bed to get the phone. Expecting Kevin's voice he is happy to hear Jeff. "Uncle Marcus?"

"Yes?"

"Hey, Dad wanted me to call and let you know we are leaving for the hospital in an hour and we will meet you there. He wanted to know if you wanted a change of clothes."

Rubbing some life back into his slack face he replies into both the phone and his hand making his voice so muffled that Jeff grunted a "huh?" back at Marcus.

"Oh, sorry, yeah, I would love a change of clothes. It doesn't matter what you bring. I will shower off before we come."

Jeff laughs, "Well I hope so, you haven't showered in like, forever. You rushed out without one two days ago… gross." Jeff ribs his Uncle.

"Right you are. I am a nasty pig… thank you for pointing it out." The smile in his voice transferring to his nephew, "We will see you soon." Marcus is surprised to see that Luis is already showered and changed, waiting serenely in the arm chair in front of the muted television, watching the news.

Sixteen minutes later Marcus and Luis are on their way out to the parking lot.

Lauren is awake and has lost some of her puffiness. Her eyes are no longer pressed slits of flesh but it did indeed look like the eyes of the girl he has known his whole life. Marcus reaches for her hand just as she reaches for his. She looks tired and can't talk. Her throat is sore from being intubated. Marcus can see the humble thanks in her eyes as she pats his hand with her own dry, swollen fingers.

Jeff and Cassie are on the bed next to her and both look relieved. The rest of the family lines the room and Marcus feels like the world is beginning to right itself. He feels as though the fabric of his life is changing, stretching to include more people and wisdom he had never considered... and he likes it. He stretches his long frame then leans down to kiss his sister. She looks slightly confused as a single tear cascades over her thick lashes.

Everyone sits and chats around the bedside until Lauren's eyes droop. Kevin ushers everyone out and they head to the cafeteria for lunch. Marcus finds himself looking around expectantly for Isadora again. He is disappointed that she is not there. He remembers that he has her card somewhere and considers rifling through his musty bundle of clothes in his back seat to find it but is instead glad to just be in something clean.

Marcus finds Jeff and rubs the back of the boys neck affectionately, feeling the tension there he says, "Hey big man, thanks for the clothes. That was your idea not your Dad's right?" Jeff looks up shyly and nods. "Don't be shy, I really appreciate it man, good looking out. Your old Uncle needs to be looked after a little sometimes. It was really nice of you to think of me." Marcus ruffles Jeff's unsettled mop and hugs him to his side as they walk. Jeff leans in without a word accepting the affection and compliments.

"You want to sit with grandpa and me at lunch?" Marcus asks Jeff.

Jeff shrugs noncommittally. Marcus smiles, "It is pretty interesting, grandpa has been telling me a story about grandma and the war and getting arrested." Jeff jerks his head up startled then his face shifts into incredulity.

"No *way*! You are kidding around again. Grandpa got arrested for what?"

Marcus leans in secretively close, "For stalking grandma." He pulls away and looks down at Jeff with a mockingly serious face. "Go ask him." Jeff looks at the stern cut of Luis's shoulders and shakes his head to the negative. Marcus laughs again, "Seriously, he isn't that bad. Old people have lived a lot and have long tales to tell. You are more than welcome to join us."

"Ok. I guess I can." Jeff says as though he is humoring his uncle.

Marcus walks to the counter to get his food. Lost in thought he is contemplating the merits of chocolate versus vanilla pudding.

"I recommend the banana." Isadora says.

Marcus's head whips up. He hadn't noticed her and felt both cheated of the chance to watch her walk in and embarrassed to be caught staring at pudding. "Uh, is that an option? I thought the signs said only chocolate and vanilla?" Marcus points at the little signs on the sneeze shield with his spoon.

"Of course banana pudding is always an option," Marcus looks around, "Just not here." She finishes.

Marcus's lips make a single thin line. He glares at her mischievously. "So you are a liar and a deceiver, aren't you Miss Trevino?"

A wide bright grin that crinkles her left eye just a bit more than her right, ignites her face. "Not and… or! I am either a liar *or* a deceiver." Marcus taps his spoon on his teeth.

"No, no, I believe you to be both." Pointing the spoon in her direction he makes a jabbing motion as though pinning her to the wall. "In fact I venture to say there are many places on this planet devoid of banana pudding, supporting the proof of your deception. I might also point out…" He waves the spoon with a flourish, "That unless you can produce some banana pudding to offer me right here and now, you are *also* a fiendish liar." Feeling proud of himself for successfully flirting, he delivers the blow to a chocolate pudding with a huge grin, suspending his spoon upright, adding the cup to his tray.

"Ah, well debated opening statement Marcus…" *She remembers my name,* he thinks as joy explodes in his head, "and yet I feel regret that you are so quick to accuse without asking for my supporting argument." She feigns a sad, dejected look. Marcus nods as though contemplating.

"Hmm, in a gesture of pure magnanimous gallantry… I entreat you for your argument…" Bowing slightly with his hand on his chest Marcus acquiesces. She laughs loud and openly. Marcus is enveloped in the sound, swimming in the fun he derives from Isadora. He has never been so flirtatious. He never even knew he could be.

Gathering her laughter Isadora locks eyes with Marcus, "I was thinking there is a place down the street that has fantastic banana pudding, I could make it up to you, show you that I am neither of the afore mentioned louts."

Marcus's tone softens as though speaking only to himself but clearly audible. "Who uses the words aforementioned and lout in the same sentence? Honestly?" Isadora glares at him, leans in and whispers as his eyes lock on her full lips, wishing the sneeze shield did not exist.

"I do."

A loud crash indicates that the rest of the world is still present in their conversation. Marcus sighs as Isadora rushes away towards the crash from the back of the kitchen, behind the wall and out of sight. He kicks the underside of the counter.

"You should have kissed her." Ricky says as he snatches a spoon from the dispenser.

Marcus growls quietly. "I should have done something!"

"Don't beat yourself up too bad, you were flirting magnificently." Marcus flushes red under his dark tan. Muttering darkly, Marcus walks back to his table.

"That is a really pretty lady you were talking to Uncle Marc." Jeff muses.

"Oh that isn't just any pretty lady Jeff," Luis says with a sly smile. Marcus's eyebrow arches in question, "that is going to be your Tia Isadora."

"Her name is Tia?" Jeff asks innocently. Marcus glares at Luis. The old man chuckles knowingly.

The three men of three different generations sit around the table enjoying each other's company. "I didn't know you were so funny Great Grandpa." Jeff says in a relaxed tone. Luis guffaws, "*You* don't know… anything… rug rat." Jeff grins.

"Uncle Marcus knew, he told me to come over and sit with you guys. He said you were telling him you got arrested for stalking great grandma." Luis shoots Marcus a withering look.

Marcus gently punches Jeff in the arm, "Hey, I told you that in confidence." Jeff grins still wider and shrugs his innocence, hands palm up.

"I did say that but only to trick you into hearing all the other great stuff he has been telling me." Marcus explains.

"Like what?" Jeff asks, curious now.

"Well sit down and I will finish. Your Uncle can catch you up later." Marcus settles onto a love seat in a brightly lit sunroom. Jeff nestles into the crook of his arm. This simple action of innocent trust and affection by Jeff makes Marcus swell inside near to bursting. *Man I love this kid,* Marcus thinks. Luis smiles proudly at them as he sits down in an arm chair in front of them.

-17-
In Kind

"I woke up in a dark corner of a dressing room off the side of the stage. I was stiff and sore and rumpled beyond that of acceptable society. Forgetting where I was and confused, I didn't immediately understand what had woke me."

"My face felt cracked and chapped, I think I must have either cried myself to sleep in sheer misery at having missed my one chance to find Janie or at least wept in my sleep. Either way I looked terrible. I felt terrible! I also knew if I didn't get off that floor and do something I was going to be in serious hot water with Uncle Sam."

"Then I heard another loud bang far off down the hall and some harsh voices. Someone was arguing and it sounded like they were throwing things as well. I didn't know what I should do. I thought I was going to be arrested as a vagrant at the very least and this time the police weren't going to be so kind."

"The only reason I even left my hiding spot was because one of the people arguing was a woman and she was distressed and crying and something in me just couldn't let anything bad happen to a woman. Not if I could do anything to prevent it or to protect her. So I brushed myself off trying to make myself as legitimate looking as possible and stepped around the corner."

"There were in fact many people standing around watching the two people argue from one room to another. At that moment they were inside one of the dressing rooms down the hall. Apparent by the crowd around the door watching the drama unfold. I felt certain that there were enough bystanders that I would not have to get involved. I lifted my collar, tried to look innocuous and made my way towards the nearest exit."

"I was sad and downtrodden. I know I looked it too, having slept in a closet in my clothes. I am certain I looked no better than a bum. I was almost out of the building when I hear a loud masculine roar. "Jane O'Brien! You will calm down and stop making a scene." I froze. That could only mean one thing to me. Ailfrid and Janie were just yards away from me. I will never forget the sound of her voice after hearing it again. It was deeper and more resonant than I remembered but it was hers.

"No father, I will not calm down! I am an adult now. I am not the girl I was two years ago… I …" She was ranting full steam ahead as she came storming out of that dressing room into the hall, but I couldn't wait another second. So I did what any gentleman would do. I interrupted her. I said… "You are more beautiful than you were two years ago." She stopped screaming and looked at my back. I hadn't turned around so she didn't know who I was. I was so nervous I was scared my legs would give out. The crowd parted between us.

"Wha…What did you say?" She asked breathless. Ailfrid hadn't yet exited the room they had been arguing in.

That is when I turned around, squared my shoulders and decided I was no longer a boy. I was a man. A man my mother and father could be proud of and I was going to take what was mine… that is if she wanted to be mine." Luis whispered as though to himself, "and I was certain she did. So I strode towards her with a purpose and hugged her to my chest as though it were possible for her to fit into the empty spot inside meant for her. She clung to me too. She looked up and cupped my face so lovingly, as if in awe, a mythical creature she had only dreamt of. "Luis?" She had asked me."

"When Ailfrid rounded the door, he lost his faculties. He pushed Janie aside and punched me in the mouth. Right there with Janie still in my arms, but I felt fortified. The pain exploding from my broken nose was barely noticeable. Everything in my world was right and good in that moment nothing was going to stop me from completion. I kissed Janie on the forehead and tucked her behind my back to protect her."

"That simple act enraged good ol' Ailfrid." Luis smiled reminiscently. "Ailfrid turned the color of a freshly boiled lobster and I swear there was actual steam coming from under his expensive collar. He railed at me. He cursed and swore and threatened. Oh and I think he punched me once more because I do remember having a split lip as well. I just stood there without moving or flinching. He lifted his hands like he was going to grab me but everything inside me hardened at once. Every muscle was firing. I think Ailfrid saw that and paused. I reached into the breast pocket above my heart and retrieved my kerchief."

"I handed it to him and said, "This is the only kiss Janie has ever given me. You raised a strong, righteous and intelligent woman Mr. O'Brien. I have loved her from the moment I saw her and never stopped for one moment in the last two years. Not for one second not in any country I was in and not when I watched the ugliness of war kill everyone around me. I loved her then and I love her now and you will not take her away from me again." Luis wipes the passion from his face and adjusts his seat in the chair.

"Wow." Exclaims Jeff, impressed.

Luis agreed. "Wow indeed young man."

Marcus shook his head slowly in amazement. "Did he hit you again?" Jeff asks.

Luis laughed. "No he did not. He wilted. He shrank. I was astounded as Janie wept silently into the center of my back. The wetness of her tears firmed my resolve. "Mr. O'Brien, Janie is coming with me and you are never going to make her cry again. If you do I will repay you in kind for the blood leaking from my face. I thought I was so gallant for that little speech, I quite impressed myself." Luis grins widely, poking Jeff in the shoulder.

"I took Janie's hand and began to lead her out. Ailfrid called after us. "You can't take care of her, you are a poor immigrant. You can't protect her or provide for her."

"That really made me angry, I think it was the hypocrisy in the thickness of his Irish brogue that got to me. I turned to him fiercely, holding back all the pain he had ever caused me and said. "I am not poor anymore, I haven't been since I came to this country and I never will be again if she will have me! The plain truth of the matter is Sir, you don't know *anything* about me, who I am or what I have accomplished in my life."

"I held Janie's hand up for him to see, held in mine. "I *will* take care of her. It isn't your job anymore sir." I turned and escorted Janie out shoving past the myriad of silent and shocked onlookers. As we neared the end of the hall a slow clap broke out and by the time the door closed behind us we were being applauded heartily. Someone had handed me back my pocket square with the kiss as we exited the building."

"You must have been super proud of yourself great grandpa?" Jeff inquires with wide eyes.

"Heck no I wasn't. What I was, was terrified. I now had a person to take care of. She was completely dependent on me and feeding her and clothing her and getting her back home to California was now my burden to bear. I was *terrified!* I was also the happiest I had ever been."

"So did ya kiss her? You did didn't you?" Jeff wrinkles his nose; his chin in his hands, fingers cradling his face.

Marcus and Luis laugh long and hard. When they recover Luis finally answers, "Yes I did son, at least once or twice, but not right then."

Jeff continues to wrinkle his nose tighter and sticks out his tongue as though he has something furry on it and says, "Blech."

Marcus ruffles the top of Jeff's head. "You are ruining the story with your maturity kiddo."

Jeff shrugs and extracts himself from the loveseat. "I am going to go check on Mom." He says, sauntering off down the hall.

-18-
Certainty

Marcus rubs his face thinking of Isadora. "Grandfather, why did you say that girl from the cafeteria is going to be Jeff's Auntie? Do you know something I don't know?"

Luis squints at Marcus as though reading a sign in a different language. "No Son, I know what you know… it is just something you either haven't recognized or don't want to."

Marcus's mouth drops open. He wants to say something to justify the gaping hole in his face but his brain is completely devoid of a response. He closes his mouth. Luis smiles knowingly. "Don't worry son, you will understand eventually. I won't let you leave here before you do." Marcus nods.

"So, why didn't you kiss her, grandma I mean?" Marcus inquires.

"Well, I had a lot on my mind. The truth is, I didn't feel like I should and she was a mess. I led her to a café where she went to the restroom to wash her face. When she returned she was calm again and I had gathered my thoughts. I said to her, "I will take you home to your mother. She will want to see you before you leave." Janie just blew on her coffee and sipped carefully. When she looked up at me, all wet lashes and big dark eyes, I wanted to kiss her then. Badly! I wanted to climb over that table and into those deep pools of certainty. Instead, I reached into my pocket and retrieved the promise ring I had carried in my pocket or on my dog tags ever since the day at the church."

"I took her delicate hand with her perfectly manicured nails into my rough work worn paw and slid that fragile little circlet in place, where it belonged."

"That is one of those moments you remember the rest of your life. It is one of the moments that have sustained me through the years. Even since she has been gone. She looked up at me and without a word she told me yes, with her eyes, it was yes to everything. Every question I could have asked her and we both knew it."

"The police did show up. The same one who had taken me to jail for loitering and just looking like a creep. When he walked into the café he had three other officers with him. When he saw it was me, he just tipped his hat to me. I stood, expecting to be handcuffed again. He sat down in my place and spoke to Janie."

"You alright miss? You look a little distressed. Is there anything I can do to help you? Is this young man the person you want to be with? When he asked that last question Janie looked up at me with shining eyes. All the love and loss and happiness I was feeling was reflected there. "Ok then young lady, I guess that answers most of my questions… apart from the one..."

"You know I always suspected that officer fella was there to see if the story Joe Schmidt had told them the night before was true. I think there was a part of each one of those officers that wanted to believe in my love story. So there they were and there we were." Luis mops his face with his handkerchief, as though out of habit more than need. He didn't look sweaty or distressed. To Marcus he just looked, in awe.

"Then to my surprise the officer says, "Is there anything I can do to help you… both of you?" When I looked down at him I could see he had tears in his eyes. I didn't know why and if I had remembered his name I would have written and asked him some years later. I wish I had told that man how much he inspired me with his belief in me and his willingness to help. Honestly, I think Janie won him over that instant she had looked at up me in response to his question and there was no other choice to it after that."

"Janie looked up at the group of men in uniform surrounding the table and said boldly, "Yes, you can find my father and ask him to come to the station and make a statement. I need him to tell you his story." The officers looked at each other bewildered.

"Just long enough for me to get home and tell my mother goodbye. She deserves as much." Janie said and then we all understood. She needed them to distract Ailfrid. She stood up and kissed them each on the cheek, thanked them and we parted ways. I cannot tell you that I was looking forward to meeting Janie's mother. If Eva was anywhere near as fierce and unyielding as Ailfrid, I was going to have a hard time getting Janie out of the house and I didn't think luck would be on my side for a second time that morning."

"It only took a short time for Janie to collect herself. She was a strong and resilient woman your grandmother. Her quiet strength was one of the things I loved about her most. She rarely raised her voice in all the years we were together. With a single look or a raised eyebrow she could quell the fiercest storm. I think even the elements were less insistent than my Janie. She was a well-mannered lady but lord she had a temper. She was a spitfire son and there was never a day in nearly sixty years that wasn't interesting. I have said it before and I will tell you again… Beauty is temporary, interesting is forever. You remember that boy. It is the main reason marriages rarely last anymore. People get married because they think they are in love when they are infatuated and they think they know someone when they have no idea if they even *like* that person as much as they *want* them." Marcus let those pearls of wisdom soak into his psyche while Luis took a breath or two. Marcus is in awe of the man before him and the cumulative wealth of wisdom he holds.

"Janie and I walked to Joe's house and collected my things. We spent an hour with Joe and his sisters. We ate and had a beer or two and that day Janie drank out of a beer bottle for the first time in her life. She took to my lifestyle with ease. I had not expected that. She came from money and privilege. I had expected her to have a much longer adjustment period. In fact, it was me that *she* had to polish up and teach the prettier manners to. She never lost her polish and shine but she never looked down her nose at any of my rough military buddies and their common, hardworking families. She wasn't judgmental as I thought rich people were. It also turned out, that *I* had been the more judgmental of the two, always trying to be a buffer between her and the rougher edges of my life and I tell you… she was tougher and kinder than I ever could have expected. She never complained or expected more than I was capable of providing. There was never any entitlement in her. Those simple qualities made me love her so devotedly that I was determined to give her the life I thought she deserved." Again, Luis removes a white stitched hankie from his shirt front and wipes his face gently, as though he is wiping something away that was much more than sheen. "So after the beer and a short rest we borrowed a car and drove to Janie's home."

"Marcus, you asked earlier what it is like to love someone, I can only tell you that it is bigger than anything you can imagine. It makes *you* bigger, wiser, more mature and imperturbable. It makes everything else seem… not as important. It just makes you a better person, not just for the person you love but for everyone who knows you. Love like I loved your grandmother, well, it is consuming. It takes every atom in your body and every bit of your soul that doesn't belong to God. Yet, it isn't a negative thing. Love fills you, all of your dark and empty spots, with light and joy. It doesn't take anything away from you, it never makes you less or ugly. If you ever think you are in love and you are acting like a fool, mean and nasty, jealous and controlling, then you aren't in love. You never want to *take* anything away from someone you love, you only want to *give*." Marcus nods, not truly knowing what Luis is talking about but fully able to understand how that could be valid.

"I understand Grandpa, thank you." Marcus says, far from lightheartedly.

Patting Marcus on the knee as though he is comforting Marcus or somehow insisting that "it" just isn't that bad, Luis smiles cajolingly. "Don't look so worried son. Janie loved me like that too. She was accustomed to a certain amount of luxury but she always said it didn't matter, she didn't want *things* she wanted *me,* and she never gave me a reason to doubt her words. She was incredible to me and I felt extremely loved. Anyhow, I get ahead of myself again… We were on our way to see Eva." Luis rubs his hands together vigorously. Marcus smiles and braces himself for what seems to be ensuing drama.

"When we got to Janie's house I have to admit to a certain amount of intimidation. They had an enormous brick Tudor home with a driveway that wrapped around nearly an acre of perfectly manicured lawn. That was just the driveway, I have no idea how much land came with the house, because there weren't any other houses in sight."

"I looked at that house and thought; I am a good man but am I good enough for this girl? I had doubts even in all off my arrogant youth and determination. I knew I could provide that kind of home for her eventually, if that is what she wanted, but I was also acutely aware that I had next to nothing to offer her in the moment. I wasn't sure I was going to be enough. To be honest, I felt so damn lucky that she was even considering me that I wasn't sure if I would *ever* be worthy of her. I was just glad she loved me back."

"You know Marcus… you should always want someone that feels lucky to be with you but doesn't feel like you are unlucky to be with them, and vice versa. *Never* think a woman is unlucky to have you, no matter how amazing she seems. If you feel like you are a good man, an honorable man, then *know* that is better than most men, whoever she is, will encounter." Again Marcus feels as though he is remiss in not taking notes. Glancing around for a napkin or scrap of paper he grits his teeth and bears down to remember; Looking as determined as a catcher in a World Series baseball game as he pounds one fist into the opposite palm.

"Calm down boy, no need for all of that angst. It turned out that Eva was nothing like her husband. She was exactly the opposite in most ways. Whereas I think Ailfrid would have happily parted my head from my shoulders, Eva seemed contented to try and drown me. She cried torrents of tears that I was worried would end up filling the house, setting us all afloat in the foyer." Luis again raked the back of his hand across his forehead, eyes wide with the memory of Eva's distress.

"She begged and pleaded and most likely dehydrated, before she resorted to pulling her fierce chignon loose… that is an old hairstyle boy… scratching her face and holding onto Janie like she was a life preserver. I have never again been so uncomfortable in my life. I continuously attempted to make Eva less manic, to reassure her and comfort her."

"My mother raised me to protect women in distress and watching Eva's heart break broke me Marcus. I am not ashamed to tell you. I loved Janie with every cell in my body but Eva managed to make me hate myself and feel guilty in every one of those cells. I offered to leave Janie for the night to appease Eva but Janie put her foot down. Literally! As she was packing her clothes she stomped her foot, turned, grasping Eva by the shoulders and shook her. I was shocked. She told her mother, "Mommy, I love him, I always have and I always will. I know what you are going to say," Janie paused allowing her head to roll as surely her eyes would have if her head remained stationary, "and it doesn't matter what he has. He is going to make me happy Mommy and that is all you ever said you wanted for me." Janie's face shone. Every inch of her skin seemed to be glowing."

"With that, Eva's sobs decreased considerably. She did continue to cry but at least it was under control. Janie had a way of stating something with so much conviction that it is as though the event to come was already fact. I didn't see the look in her eyes but I knew that tone of voice from the cafe and knew how futile it would be to try and argue with it. I think her mother must have known that look and that level of determination much better than I did."

-19-
Impending

"That afternoon I drove back to Joe's and we stayed through the day enjoying the company of his family. It was a hectic day for me. The certainty of knowing she was with me, that she was mine and that *I* was no longer *me*... from that day forward *I* had become *we*, combined with the need to put my future in motion had me frayed and sparking like a downed wire in water." Marcus smiles, imagining Luis's stress level to be like the moment before a tipoff in an important game.

"Later in the evening I ran an errand or two, leaving Janie with Joe's sisters. The most important of which was Janie's bus ticket. I was taking her with me back to California and I didn't care what I had to do to make it all work. I used the last of my savings and the precious few favors I had left to get her on that military transport. I sent my mother a letter, hoping it would precede Janie and me by a few days and give my mother time to prepare for our arrival. I wasn't looking forward to facing my mother's wrath and confusion but I knew she would eventually love Janie as I do." Marcus noticed the telling present tense of the word "do" as opposed to the use of the word "did;" admiring Luis's current love for his long dead wife.

"I returned with Janie's ticket and a bunch of daisies and sunflowers for Joe's family, one of Joe's sisters helped me put them in a vase. While we were alone in the kitchen she said to me, "You know… I was hoping I had a chance with you Luis… You are such a good and kind man…" She placed the flowers on the Formica table and grabbed me by the lapels of my shirt, rose up on her tiptoes and kissed me on the cheek, "but I can see you belong to Janie. No one else will have a chance and I would be jealous but she really is incredible. I would dislike her if I couldn't help liking her so much." I was stunned and terrified that someone would walk in and misunderstand the situation."

"Someone did walk in. Janie walked in and we froze. I thought she would leave me then and there. I thought so many things at once that all I could do was stutter, making me look only guiltier still. I will tell you boy, in that moment I felt more true terror than I ever had on the battlefield being shot at and watching my buddies die." Marcus's eyes shot open feeling a nervous angst on behalf of his grandfather.

"All Janie did was stroll up to Joe's sister, removed her hands from my shirt front gently and held them in her own, kissed the smaller girl on the cheek and said warmly. "Thank you so much for your kindness and hospitality." The girl had tears in her eyes as she said, "I hope to have what you and Luis have one day. I hope to have a love so certain. Good luck in your life you two." She hugged us both quickly and although we kept in contact with Joe, we never saw her again."

Marcus let loose of a long sigh, "I know how that girl felt. I think everyone who doesn't have that wants it." Luis chuckles softly next to Marcus's sullen face.

"An hour before we were supposed to be at the bus station Janie asked me if she could go see her father. She had misgivings about leaving without ever speaking to him again. She had called him and asked him to meet her at the church where they had been going since they arrived in New York. The Church was only blocks from the bus station that had the military transports."

"Yes, I see the look on your face Marcus. It must have been the same look of skepticism and fear that had been on my own face. Yet, Janie trusted that her father would not do anything rash inside the church."

"I begged her not to go but she just gave me that all knowing look that said we were forever and I couldn't refuse her."

"Joe took us first to the church and dropped her off where she gave me a kiss that felt like all the promise I could ever have asked for, squeezed my hand and left me in charge of her bags. When she topped the steps in front of the church, a priest opened the door for her and gave me a wave, as though he knew me and was assuring me she was going to be in safe hands. I then remembered how great Father James had been and felt a little less anxiety. She looked back at me as her full skirts disappeared with her behind those massive ornate doors."

"Joe then took me to the bus station where I checked in our bags and confirmed our travel plans with the ticket master. I know it doesn't sound like a good time son, but I was looking forward to our four day trip back to California. It was going to be the longest time I was going to be alone with her and I couldn't wait to just sit there, next to her and feel her hand in mine and the heat of her head on my shoulder as we rode. I was beside myself with joy."

"Then the hour was gone and the last call was being heralded. Janie was nowhere to be seen. Joe had already left and went to the church to pick Janie up as soon as we had started boarding. I asked two old sergeants, waiting out their last few months for their retirement as the military liaison in the bus station and the driver of the bus to hold the bus but the driver said, "Son, you get off this bus and I am closing those doors, you will have to catch the bus the next week and I am sure your commanding officer likes AWOL privates as much as mine does. I will give you five more minutes then I will have you removed if you don't settle down.""

"That is when Joe arrived breathless and sweating, clothes rumpled, yelling through the terminal; "They took her, they took her, I don't know who it was but they wouldn't let me in the church and I saw them taking her. She didn't want to go Luis." The driver closed the door in Joes face and three officers next to me held me down until my strength to struggle failed me. The last thing I heard was Joe running behind the bus yelling, "She didn't want to go."

Marcus felt the chill of the moment in the wetness of unspent tears threatening to run over, recognizing the agony his grandfather was reliving in the telling of his story.

-20-
Determination

"The Officer seated next to me was Ezekiel Jordan. A newly promoted Captain that was much older than a new Captain usually was. He was a tall powerful, dark skinned man that spoke in a slow educated drawl. He told me his story on the second day of our trip when he noticed I hadn't moved let alone eaten or drank anything since we left. I think I would have cried like a baby Marcus if I hadn't been so damn angry at having been so close to happiness and having it slip through my fingers."

"Ezekiel explained that he too had once been deeply in love and he too had fought for his girl, a girl whose father would never have allowed her to be with a black man. Ezekiel's love had been a Caucasian girl and their separation was racial more than religious or financial."

"He showed me the scars his chiseled face bore from the beatings that her father and his friends had given him on several occasions. Eventually her father had him framed for stealing something from one of his friends and when he went to court the judge had given him a choice between life in the military and life in prison." Looking up to the surprised inhale from Marcus, Luis continued, "Ah yes, it was unfair, but those were different times and the depth of your skin color was in direct correlation to how much justice you would get, and Ezekiel was nearly ebony dark."

"I can tell you, I have never seen a man so striking in uniform with his handsomely scared face, imposing posture and slight limp in his march. His defining feature though, was the deep sadness in his eyes that never left even when he laughed. Ezekiel and I ended up being great friends even though he was much older, much higher ranking and despite the fact that he tried his hardest the entire trip to convince me to give up on Janie."

"Ezekiel was the man who inspired me to get my education. He is the one that convinced me to use the Military and the system of oppression we lived in to further my advancement. I never did give up on Janie though. I knew that I had found her once. I could find her again. I had Joe and all his friends and contacts in New York looking for her but she had disappeared off of the Follies poster and was never seen at the theater again. I like to think Janie is the reason Joe was happily married for fifty-two years when he passed. He ended up dating and marrying a makeup girl that worked in the theater. She was a great lady that treated him well and kept him happy until the end. They even had seven kids." Luis laughed and shook his head. "Joe became a butcher when he got out of the Army and opened his own shop on the Bronx. He did well for himself and his family and was a great help to me in my search for Janie."

"Joe's shop put him in contact with many different people, to include the Italian Mafia and the Hasidic Jews that came to

Joes shop for the kosher meats the Joe became known for. It was those contacts that finally gave me a ray of light into my search for Janie. Joe and I exchanged a great many letters and calls through the years so I always had some sort idea where your grandmother was and that she was safe and healthy. It was all rumor that Joe overheard in the shop, but it was better than nothing."

Luis pats Marcus on the knee as was becoming his custom and stood. "Are you thirsty son? My throat is dry from all this talking. Mayhap my tongue will glue to the roof of my mouth if I don't give it a rest."

Marcus stood and stretched, smiling wryly. "Let's walk Grandpa, I feel like I am getting old." Luis guffaws and laughs a deep throaty chuckle that reminds Marcus of an actor that narrates documentaries.

"You know son, I think I did cry, maybe not with tears but I stared out that bus window seeing nothing for what seemed like days before Ezekiel reached me through my fog of pain. I remember seeing landscapes change and the sun come up and go down a few times, even the thick inky black darkness of the land at night where there were no streetlights. It is a long drive from New York City to Camp Pendleton California. I think I must have been crying inside all that time because I remember little else about that trip."

Marcus stops to still his grandfather's forward progression with a gentle hand on his shoulder. "But wait, what happened to Grandma? Did you guys ever talk about what happened to her?"

-21-
Struck

"Oh yes son, we talked about it, but I think there is someone *you* should be talking to. I need to excuse myself."

Marcus looks up in confusion and scans the room expecting to see Jeff but recognizes no one in the room. Stretching again groaning softly he leans to pick up the food trays from the table.

A soft voice from behind him says, "Interesting." Marcus starts and knocks a handful of napkins to the floor, he stumbles over a chair to catch them in mid-flight.

A deft hand seems to materialize from thin air to pluck a few floating napkins from the air as though she is performing a Chinese kerchief trick. Wow, he thinks, she is so graceful, mesmerized by the flow of her skirt and how it seems to perfectly match the rhythm of the falling napkins. The motion of her swift arms wafting her warm summer scent in his direction as she smoothly negotiates around the table to pick up the remaining napkins from the floor. She is looking down at the ground and Marcus can only see the crown of her glossy head, glad that she cannot see how abashed he feels as he rearranges the full trays.

"Isadora?" Marcus asks more softly than he intended.

She looks up and all he can see is the liquid shimmer of her large languidly exotic eyes. Something explodes inside his stomach, something that feels dangerous, not in a gastrointestinal way but much the same as it felt when he decided to go bungee jumping with his buddies in college. His insides flip over and his heart begins to race with what only can be described as hope, joy and happiness all at once.

Isadora opens her mouth to respond but pauses before sound comes out as she experiences butterflies of her own looking up at Marcus so tall and handsome with a kind of goofy look on his chiseled face and one hand in his pocket like a little kid. Her breath catches as she hears him say, almost as though he is telling someone a secret, *"So this is it."* Then shakes his head thinking of the many descriptions his father had shared with him.

"What is… it?" Isadora asks as she stands.

"What?" Marcus says, confused. "Oh I meant pudding," Isadora is now confused as well. She frowns causing her forehead to form a single delicate crease just to the right of her left eyebrow. Marcus smiles because he is astounded by how cute it is but her confusion turns to indignation.

"Are you talking in riddles on purpose or just playing with me." Her hand finding its way to her hip.

"Oh, no I was just thinking out loud, I am sorry," Without taking a breath to pause he flows directly into, "When do you get off work?" He asks looking at his watch noticing that it is still early but wanting to be with her now, this minute and wishing he could take her, anywhere, right now.

Isadora just looks at him in amazement. She is reeling with the speed at which he changed tacks.

"Uh…" She begins as she walks beside him to the trash receptacle "are you asking me out?" She knows the answer to this, she is just playing for time to gather her emotions.

Marcus takes hold of her hand gently and looks at her so sincerely and with so much mischief her butterflies take flight again. "No, I am not." She frowns again as her cheeks heat. "I am accepting your… forward invitation from earlier." Realization breaks across her face, causing her to giggle. Marcus straightens as she smiles. "I would love some banana pudding."

"*Meeee too!*" Luis smacks his lips and rubs his belly as he returns to Marcus's side.

"Great, it's a date then." Marcus says.

"Oh-ho, not for this old man. Are you ready to go see Lauren? I suppose I have been taking up plenty of your time and you didn't come all the way here to have me talk your ear off. You are here for your sister."

Isadora hands Marcus a folded napkin and squeezes his hand, "I get off at five. I will be hungry," before she strides purposefully back towards the kitchen, her full skirt swaying seductively around her hips.

Opening the napkin Marcus reads; *Meet me in the front lobby at 5:30.* Next to the graceful script is a kiss. Marcus smiles all the way to his toes. Stuffing the note in his pocket he turns his attention to his family.

Luis whistles low. "Look at that walk. I love a pretty girl that knows what she wants and speaks her mind, Marcus. My Janie has been gone a while now, you better be careful or I might put the old charm on that beauty." Luis shuffles a few steps in a staggered formation, "I can still dance you know, and the ladies love that." Marcus laughs good-naturedly.

"Ok grandpa, lay off, you have to give me a chance, I am pretty new to this whole chivalry thing." Marcus puts his arm across Luis's shoulders and they walk out just as Jeff skips up.

"Mom is breathing on her own now, no machine." Luis claps, Marcus whoops and Jeff lifts Marcus's free arm up and rests it on his own shoulders.

Marcus feels buoyant on the long walk down the hall to Lauren's room.

-22-
Inevitability

She said she gets off at five, Marcus thinks as he waits in the main entry to the hospital. Looking at his watch for at least the twentieth time in the last thirteen minutes. "I need to calm down. She said five-thirty." He mumbles quietly. Thinking Isadora may have stood him up but doubting it every time he closes his eyes and remembers the expression on her face as she gazed up at him in the cafeteria. There had been so much honesty and sincerity there. Those big tawny eyes like deep pools of the richest orange pekoe tea. Pools that open and flicker shut with mysteries that felt tailor made to him. His stomach begins to canter at the thought yet again.

Marcus begins to pace, just to have something to do with his body. Typically if he were home and feeling this anxious he would drop to the floor and do a hundred push-ups or maybe some sit-ups. Probably not a good idea to do something like that in public, he considers, she would think I am one of those fitness idiots that brings protein bars on dates.

"Considering bolting?" Isadora asks jovially.

Marcus spins on one heel trying to locate the origin of her voice. "Nope, was thinking maybe you had?"

Isadora looks at her feet, "Yes, well I am usually prompt or at least considerate enough to have called to let you know, but I don't have your number," She lifts her eyes, pinning him with warmth, "Yet." She glares playfully at him. "Besides, I am early so shut your face." They both laugh.

Marcus reaches, "Your hands are full may I help?"

A small frown flits across her brow to disappear as quickly as it had come. "Thank you that would be most helpful. This stuff can get heavy." She hands him a large stack of paper. "These are all suggestions from patients and visitors as to what can be improved in the food service here at the hospital."

Marcus cringes, "Over what time frame, this can't be one day's worth?" She laughs.

"No, that is a week's worth, seems people in hospital beds have nothing better to do than complain about the food." She shrugs.

Marcus makes a face similar to a Muppet, his mouth going wide and thin. "Well, honestly I never have heard anything good about the food in any hospital. Have you?"

She laughs again, he notices that laughter comes easily to her. He likes that. So many women are so self-conscious and take themselves so seriously. Isadora seems so unassuming and comfortable, even confident.

"No, I haven't, not in a regular hospital. In private care it is a different story. Money makes the difference." She frowns a real frown, full of concern and depth. "Anyway, we are here, this is my car." Marcus hadn't even realized they had been walking, let alone having exited the building.

"If you would just put that stack in the trunk please. There is a box marked suggestions."

Marcus responds to the click of the trunk as she remotely opens it. It springs open to reveal an astoundingly organized picture of how her mind works. There are several boxes with labels, and emergency road side kit, tools and a basketball suspended in a cargo net. Yet the trunk itself doesn't even have a crumb in it. She is obviously a fastidious person. Another trait that deeply appeals to Marcus. The fact that she has a basketball makes sparks of joy go off inside his head.

He is about to comment when she interrupts his thoughts, "So am I driving or are you? It isn't far, we could even walk."

"It is nice out, let's walk." Isadora's face lights up, causing her tawny eyes to glint. Marcus's stomach quickens.

"Yay, it feels so good to be out of the back halls, breathing fresh air." She is obviously overjoyed her day is over and her energy is infectious. Marcus finds himself smiling for no reason of his own.

"So the outcome is bright?" She asks.

"I'm sorry… I am not sure…" Marcus begins.

She laughs again, "Oh you mean you aren't actually inside my head reading my thoughts?" She laughs at her own presumption. "I meant with your sister, I do that all the time, transition from thought into words without considering context." Marcus smiles as he offers her his hand to walk across the intersection. She accepts happily, smiling broadly at the unexpected chivalry.

"Thank you for being such a gentlemen, it is rare that a gorgeous man is so polite. I deeply admire that."

"Oh, of course, you are welcome, it isn't often such a stunning girl is so appreciative." Isadora looks boldly into his eyes, catching them both in mid-step, stopping as one. Marcus stares down, the silence heavy.

He turns as abruptly physically as he is internally from his thoughts of wanting to kiss her. "My sister, Lauren, is doing much better. We are all very relieved. She is my only sister and while we have our differences, I love her and her kids, I can't imagine not getting horrid Christmas cards from her or worthless messages about her beagle." Isadora makes a sound just short of an audible laugh. A look of concerned contemplation on her perfect features.

"What? No laugh? I was hoping to hear that all night." She looks up.

"Why?"

"I like it, your laugh makes me happy. It makes me want to laugh too." Isadora looks at him is shock.

"Is that hubris flowing from your mouth right now? Are you actually just saying what you think?" She inquires challengingly.

"Why yes, Miss Trevino, I am… problem?"

"Nope. Not from me. I think I might just be in love, you haven't once asked me what a word means, and as you covertly pointed out earlier, I have used quite a few scrabble words on you already." She grins and waves her finger at him as though he has been caught being naughty.

"You heard that, did you?" He chuckles, considering seriously how much he might enjoy this woman being in love with him. "Well slow down, no proposals yet, I am certain there are other things about me that will convince you that I swim in the shallower end of the DNA pool." She does laugh heartily this time.

"No good trying to put me off, I have seen your family and they are quite a bunch of specimens. You might be one of the lesser, but still impressive, although… your Father is quite a looker. Very much the burly Sam Elliot. Every lady loves Sam

Elliot." She plucks a leaf off a tree and tosses it at Marcus. Now he is laughing too.

"I could introduce you to him if you like but I warn you… he claims that his house is overrun with barking spiders… and when they bark it smells horrendous." They both laugh all the way into the little dessert shop, making the patrons all look towards the door as they enter.

Noticing the stares they sober slightly. Holding on to his arm for stability, Isadora rises on tip-toe to whisper in his ear, "I take back the accusation of gentlemanly manners, what gentleman talks about flatulence on the first date?" Marcus laughs as her words caress the skin behind his ear. He turns to look at her glittering eyes and then at her lips, she licks them nervously, looking at his as well.

"Can I help you folks?" A stout man in a white apron and cap asks from behind the counter.

"Uh, yes, we would like two banana puddings please." Isadora says without breaking eye contact with Marcus.

"How long have you two been together?" A pretty teenage girl asks from behind the counter. She must be the stout man's daughter, as she has the same pug nose and bright crystal blue eyes.

"Us?" Marcus asks, indicating his chest then Isadora's with a fingertip. "Forever… like a million years right babe?" Isadora chokes, but recovers, playing along.

"Oh yes, since we were what," She looks to Marcus with wide eyes, trying to invent, "four?" She finishes, hoping that her dishonesty isn't absurdly transparent. The girl just shifts her weight to one foot, a glazed doe eyed expression of romanticism on her face.

"Aw, that is so cute. That is a *really looooong* time." Marcus's face falls as the girl stretches out the word long.

"Hey, not *that* long." He states.

Isadora snickers into her palm. Marcus takes the tray and pays, leaving a generous tip.

"Thanks Mr." The boy at the register says happily.
The couple finds a secluded booth with their banana pudding. After a few bites in silence Isadora entreats, "So? What do you think? Any good?"

"Honestly? I make better!" Marcus teases.

"What? Seriously?" She feigns incredulity.

Marcus scoops up a spoonful and eats it. "Well, maybe yours isn't as good as mine," She scoops some of his pudding out and eats it, "nope, same as mine."

"What? Did you honestly just do that?" He laughs "Greedy aren't you? You just want mine and yours." He spoons a dollop of her pudding onto his spoon, and pulls it towards his mouth then spins the spoon, depositing the dollop on the tip of her nose.

Isadora freezes. Speaking carefully, trying not to laugh she says, "I am scared to move, please get it off, before it drips on my shirt, it will stain."

Marcus reaches for his napkin, then leans in and kisses and nibbles the pudding off the tip of her nose. Finished, he leans back a fraction of the distance between them and looks into her eyes. All laughter and playfulness have drained from them to be replaced by something deep and mysterious, smoldering and heated. Not quite passion or wanting, something richer.

Isadora's heart is racing. How can I be *this* comfortable with someone I don't even know? Why does this feel like coming home? Why do I actually *feel* like we have been together since we were children? How can this be happening *now?*

After all I have been through and everything I left behind, how can I be feeling this? Numerous thoughts twirl in her brain making her second guess this moment and she says, "It would have been twenty-two years for me." Thinking back to the comment the girl at the counter had made about them being together since they were four. She had to say *something, anything,* to distract her from wanting Marcus to kiss her.

Marcus didn't miss a beat this time, the moment was too aligned, they were too in tune, he knew exactly where her thoughts were and what she meant by the statement, "They would have to of been an incredible twenty-two years." He whispers and kisses her ever so softly at first feeling the silken texture of her lips, inhaling the scent of her skin mingled with the sweet taste of the banana pudding, he feels intoxicated. He doesn't pull away from the chaste kiss until her breath catches in her throat. Pulling away he now knows *exactly* what his father was talking about. His entire body and his mind have ignited with possibility and joy.

"Are you ok?" He asks Isadora, noticing that she hasn't spoken a word or made a sound other than labored breathing. "I didn't overstr…" His words are cut off by her more urgent kiss. His face held firmly in place by her hand caressing his jaw with her thumb as her fingers kneed his neck. It is both passionate and nurturing but intensely driven. Marcus is stunned happy.

"Aw, you guys are so awesome. How cute are you? PDA is so great when it is like, real, not all gross and gropey." The girl has come to collect their cups and trays, startling both Isadora and Marcus out of their moment.

Marcus sits back and mouths silently to Isadora, "P…D…A?" She smiles. When the girl leaves she says, "Public Displays of Affection. Her family must be military somewhere along the line."

Marcus leans back putting one arm around her and one on the back rest. "Yes sweetling, I know what it means but she said it so condescendingly." He laughs.

Isadora beams, "Indeed she did. Sweetling?" she inquires.

Marcus shrugs kissing the side of her forehead, "Yeah, I don't know where that came from, it just seemed to fit." She shrugs as well, accepting the term of endearment. Marcus slides from the booth offering his hand, to help her up.

As they walk out, she reaches for one of the doors but unseen, Marcus holds the top of the door so that she cannot open it while opening the other door for her, causing her to divert to the other door he is holding open. He just smiles and lets her think the door she tried was locked. Marcus enjoys an independent woman and likes this one enough to let her keep thinking she is, but he *will* open every door for her when they are together, because tonight, she opened a door for him, inside him that he was beginning to believe didn't exist.

As they walk back to the parking lot Marcus has his arm casually slung around her shoulders, she rests her head in the crook of his shoulder as she is just about perfectly shoulder height. They chat intermittently. In between sentences Marcus would kiss her softly on her forehead or temple, anywhere his lips happened to land as they stroll.

He is in shock how easy it is to be with her. He reflects in the quiet moments how they both just seem to fall in next to each other. There was no need to worry about who likes who more, or if he was doing or saying the right thing. Everything just fit.

When they arrive at the parking lot Isadora stops, still half a parking lot from her car. Turning to Marcus she has an earnest expression when she says, "I don't expect anything you know? I am just going to enjoy you while you are here. I know you will be leaving soon." Marcus begins to speak, wanting to reassure her of his intentions, but she raises her hand to still him. "You don't have to say anything, I know you like me. I like you too. Tonight has felt like we jumped ahead those twenty-two years and it feels good and right. We both know this is special and we are both aware that it won't last much longer. So let's just have as much fun as we can, Okay?"

Marcus is shaking his head in the negative for the entire speech then begins to shake his head in accent with her last sentence. He smiles a sad smile looking into her eyes, nearly garnet colored in the dark. "Ok sweetling. We will talk more about it another day. For now, you are going to let me walk you to your car and you are going to let me kiss you deeply and for many long moments," He can't hold back the grin, "then you are going to go home and dream of me as though there is no real life to consider." He turns her to face her car, places his hand in the small of her back and gestures with his other hand for her to walk. After a few steps falling back into their comfortable joined stroll.

"You know? I usually do the bossing, not the other way around." Isadora teases.

"Oh, I am sure that is true, but I wasn't bossing you, I was stating fact." She pokes him in the ribs and he winces.

When they reach the car, Isadora unlocks the door but Marcus puts his hand on her shoulder when she reaches for the handle. "I will get that." He says a little more commanding than he intended, but she only smiles.

"I should apologize for my lack of etiquette but the plain fact is, I have either been alone or dated men who didn't open doors. Women as independent as I am usually get treated like we don't need a man to be chivalrous. We do, so I will try harder to let you." Marcus nods.

"Deal." He holds on to her shoulder then slides his hand down to her bicep. "You forgot something."

Pulling her into his chest like a ballroom dance veteran, she laughs in surprise. He holds her tightly and urgently then releases her to hold her gently to him, reaching up with both hands he smooth's her soft wavy hair from both sides of her face. Lifting her face she thinks he is going to kiss her but his head drops to her jaw, then lower, his nose grazes the tender flesh of her throat and she can feel and hear him inhale.

He doesn't know what makes him act this way with Isadora but he just wants to know her intricately, her fragrance, the texture of her skin, the sound of her breath near his ear. He trails his nose from where her collarbone meets her neck to the cleft behind her ear, across her cheek to find her mouth slightly parted and moist when he finally claims her lips. She gasps as he brushes his lips across hers before slowly and methodically tasting every inch of her top and bottom lip massaging them with his own. Biting and tugging with his teeth his tongue enters her mouth deftly in the most intimate kiss she has ever shared. She feels as though he is kissing her every atom at once and it is incredible.

Marcus is on fire. Not with carnal sexuality or desire, but with pure ravenous hope as he closes the car door for her and watches her drive away. He knows in this moment, his life has changed. He is now an addict. He will for the rest of his life be chasing the feeling he has right now, the feeling that Isadora gave him for the last five hours is a feeling he can't live without.

"I can't wait to tell the old man." Marcus isn't thinking of Kellan, he is of course thinking of Luis. He half runs half dances and even skips a step or two to his truck. Sliding in behind the wheel Marcus is riding adrenaline that far surpasses any basketball game he has ever played. "Damn it, I forgot to ask her about the ball in the trunk."

Isadora in turn is glowing, she too is filled with an energy that makes her feel like she is about to spontaneously combust. She is smiling so broadly that she is afraid her cheeks will split, they are certainly tiring from the involuntary strain. She shakes her head trying to clear away the blinding brilliance of fireworks behind her eyes.

It takes her an hour to get home taking the long route that had been designated by the police as the safest and hardest route to follow. She has to be up at five in the morning but she doubts she will be able to sleep.

Pulling up to the high security parking garage of her building, she takes her gun out of her purse, chambers a round, switches the safety off and rolls down the window just enough to punch in her code. Rolling up the window immediately she holds the gun, finger on the trigger until she pulls into the garage and the metal security door closes safely behind her.

Looking around the car just in case, she opens the door, gun still in hand and pops the trunk with her keys. "I may as well get started on sorting those damn suggestions. I won't be sleeping for a while tonight." She mumbles guardedly but unable to completely conceal her joy. She walks smiling to the elevator unaware that a shadow casts on the security door from the outside.

A faceless shadow watches from behind the strong metal slats that make up the door.

-23-
Timing

"Why are you going on and on about this son?" Luis is trying to keep his smug smirk under control as Marcus paces excitedly back and forth.

Marcus pauses looking at his grandfather with a confused frown. It feels so foreign to his facial muscles after falling asleep and waking up with a smile on his face. He smiles all the way through breakfast, prompting Cassie to ask him what was so funny, several times and leading Jeff to suggest that he just has gas. A statement that made Cassie giggle for nearly five minutes after Jeff left the room to check on his mother.

"What do you mean?" Marcus asks. "This is supposed to be one of the greatest moments of my life, according to dad and according to you." Marcus throws his arm up and points at Luis accusingly.

Luis erupts in deep laughter at the obvious discomfort of his tall handsomely tousled grandson. "You know your shirt is inside out don't you son?" Marcus looks at his shirt sleeve, noticing the stitched seaming is indeed on the outside. Sliding his hand to the collar front to pull the shirt over his head he can feel the tag. "And backwards." Luis completes his thought.

Ricky enters as Marcus shrugs out of his shirt reversing it in the process. "Are we getting naked in hospitals now? Is that some sort of native ritual you never taught me dad?" He chuckles. "Marcus, you look like a special kind of mess. What's going on in here?"

"The boy is telling me *his* love story now." Luis chides.

"What? I didn't say I was in love, I was just telling you about my date with Isadora." Marcus stands with his hands palm forward as though he were pleading his case.

Ricky pats Marcus on the shoulder. "You are showing all the signs." Ricky motions to the shirt still in Marcus's hand. Marcus stammers, incredulous, but inarguably caught, he clinches his lips tight. Ricky chuckles low in his throat.

"Why are you looking so smug dad?"

Luis smiles knowingly. "Because I was wondering how long it was going to take this kid to figure out what we already knew."

Ricky nods. "Yeah, it *was* pretty blatant Marcus."

Marcus finally speaks wearily, almost afraid to ask. "What are you two talking about?"

"We are talking about you and Isadora. It was obvious in the cafeteria that you both liked each other. There was something special there. You could just see it." Ricky grips Marcus's shoulder again, this time firmly. "Buck up boy, life is grand, love is grand and you finally get your chance… at what thirty?"

Marcus scowls. "I'm not yet thirty, thank you."

Jeff enters, the little waiting room they have all grown accustomed too. "Hey everyone, good news, the Docs have good news… Oh hey, Uncle Marc, finally noticed your shirt was messed up huh?" He nods at his shirtless uncle. Marcus scrambles to put the shirt on, this time correctly.

"You could have told me you little mutant."

"No fun that way, come on." Jeff grabs Marcus's wrist to pull him towards the open door.

The other two men follow them to Lauren's room. Kevin and Cassie are already there and Lauren is awake. She is groggy and unable to speak above a whisper from being intubated for so many days, but she smiles weakly at everyone.

The team of doctors go into a lengthy explanation of the ongoing and future care Lauren will require. They expect her to recover to a nearly normal way of life but that she will always be weaker and more susceptible to illness than she had been previously.

Marcus listens closely but never takes his eyes from his sister's face, watching her fade in and out of restless sleep. She looks so weak, it is hard for him to see her this way but he does feel a tremendous weight lift as the doctor reassures them that she is "mostly out of danger."

After the long discourse everyone trickles from the small room into the hallway. "Let's go get a milkshake Uncle Marc." Jeff winks at Marcus, uplifted from the news that his mother will eventually be coming home. Kellan joins them without a word and walks with his arm around Marcus giving him the customary, *dad side hug* with one arm.

"Me too Dad. I feel better now but I am still worried. Did I just miss it or did the doctor not specify how much longer Lauren will be here?"

"No one really stated an estimate. Probably some legal jargon or something, you know doctors don't ever know anything exactly. Sorry kid." Kellan ads for Jeff's sake.

Jeff skips ahead of them and turns around, skipping backwards in front of them. "Something is better than nothing right?" Marcus nods his agreement, happy that Jeff is happy.

"You have to admire the hope and resilience of kids." Kellan comments as they enter the cafeteria.

Marcus scans the room looking for Isadora. He doesn't see her and is disquieted by this. It just occurs to him that Lauren's health has a direct correlation to the amount of time he will get with Isadora. He has the unworthy thought that hopefully Lauren will recover slowly. He shakes himself internally ashamed of his selfishness.

In truth, that isn't entirely accurate. Even if Lauren wasn't out of the woods so to speak, Marcus needs to return to Vegas as soon as possible. His new job had only let him leave without pay because his sister was supposed to be near death's door.

Marcus begins to consider the amount of time he was going to be able to spend with Isadora and at best it was no more than three days. That realization made Marcus's heart race as though he were somehow scared of something. For the first time in his life he is scared to lose something even if he wasn't quite certain of what that something was.

Marcus remembers a line from a poem that he had heard at a poetry reading in a lounge in college:

In order to love, one must realize the risk of loss
What greater loss than having had not
Ever to feel that which completes you
Destiny doesn't search, you have to reach through

Marcus makes up his mind instantly. He isn't going to leave it up to fate; he is going to do whatever he has to do to help this thing with Isadora grow. He knows now he wants it to grow. He doesn't want to walk away without knowing what it could become. It is more than fun, more than passion. He knows that she is *the one.* She is the woman that has made him feel and value and desire longevity and completion.

Determined to find Isadora he strides from the cafeteria to find her office.

-24-
Coincidences?

Isadora is not at the Hospital.

Isadora is having her car towed along with two other residents of her high rise. There had been sharp metal fragments spread all over the garage driveway and it caused all four tires to go flat.

They also had to fill out insurance claims with the building management and her car insurance company. The security manager was with the police attempting to find some recorded evidence of what had happened to the drive.

Security had called the police because there was no way the shards could have been an accident. If the shards had been limited to the one garage entrance then it would be believable that the metal had been accidentally dropped from a construction truck, or some other sort of industrial accident.

However, the shards had been at every car entrance to the garage. Someone had intentionally targeted her building with the intention to cause damage.

This information made Isadora warily uncomfortable. She has a nagging feeling that she has been targeted specifically, but she was trying to talk herself out of that thought process.

When she had been relocated they had assured her that there was no way for her past to have followed her to San Francisco. She had been moved to the Bay Area because she had no family and no ties to the city itself. Yet she couldn't get the hair on the back of her neck to go down. She kept looking over her shoulder expecting to see some hulking figure skulking in the shadows. The unease in her every muscle makes her feel like her intuition is stronger than her trust of the authorities.

"Ma'am?" A short police woman in a black uniform was talking to her and apparently had been for a while. "Ma'am? Are you okay?"

Isadora shakes her head. "Uh yeah, sorry, I was just worried about getting to work."

"Oh?" The blonde hard faced officer asks suspiciously, "That is exactly what I was saying." "There is an officer across the street waiting to take you, and he will be taking you home tonight if you need a ride." She stares into Isadora's face. "Any idea why you are the only person in this building getting a police escort?"

Isadora looks at the woman's badge, noting her last name and badge number, distrust emanating from her every word. "No, officer… George, I don't know why? If you don't maybe you should ask your commanding officer." Officer George glares at Isadora, disbelief etched on the cracked lines of her face and points towards the unmarked police car with the officer in plain clothes.

When Isadora arrives at the car, the officer opens the door for her and locks her in. "Am I in some sort of trouble?" she asks as he fastens his seatbelt.

"No Miss you are not, this is for your protection. We got a call from the state department right after your building security called in the complaint. You are to be escorted to work and I will be waiting for you at the Hospital until you needed to go home. I am to stay on premises at all times."

Isadora sighs and melts into the leather seat, her hand on her chin, her elbow on the door handle, looking forlornly out the darkened window.

"For how long Officer…"

"Denis."

"For how long officer Denis? Is this just for today?" She asks thinking of Marcus and her already limited time with him. This may put an abrupt end to their short tryst. Her shoulders drop as she thinks, *this is more than a tryst Isa and you know it.*

"No Ma'am, I am afraid not, they didn't give me an end date. In fact they didn't even tell me why I am escorting you. I am just doing what I am told." Officer Denise explains via rear view mirror eye contact.

James Denis is tall and has the slightly ill-fitting look of a regular off the rack department store shopper. His blue button up shirt is a little too loose for his sleeves to be the inch short too short that shows his wrists. He sits ram rod straight in the driver's seat with his long neck extended in a painfully erect manner. He looks disciplined but slightly uncomfortable in what Isadora guesses to be a newly acquired plain clothes position.

The drive to the Hospital takes an hour when it usually took only ten to fifteen minutes. "Uh, Officer De.." He interrupts her. "You can call me James, that is my first name or you can call me *Detective* Denis, whichever you prefer." Isadora frowns considering his sentence.

"So… James, since we are going to be seeing a bit of each other, can we be friends?" She asks tentatively.

Officer Denis's face hardens for an instant with a flicker of anger and sadness, but it is gone before it truly materializes. "To be honest Ma'am, I don't have many friends," Isadora turns to look out the window, noticing that they are circling a block a few blocks down from the hospital. Her attention returns to her escort as she hears him mumble almost inaudibly, "most of them are gone." She assumes he is a combat veteran.

Unaware that her thoughts pass her lips she whispers, "Mine too." Officer Denis looks at the pretty woman in his back seat through the mirror again and witnesses her sadness silently, wondering who she really is and what she is involved in. His instructions to take her to work have come through his ear piece.

Marcus is on the front lawn of the Hospital in a crowd of visitors and staff, that had been evacuated due to what had been described as a routine inspection. Unnoticed Officer Denis opens the door of the unmarked car for Isadora. She slides out quickly spotting Marcus immediately and internally praying that he doesn't turn around and see her, or Officer Denis. She isn't ready to explain her past to Marcus yet. *With any luck, he will leave town before I have too.* She hopes silently.

Marcus turns just before Isadora sneaks up behind him, catching her in the process. She suddenly feels, happy, content and light for the first time in hours. Just seeing him smile at her makes her entire world feel right and safe. She rushes to him and buries her face in his chest, near tears of relief and not wanting him to sense her strain and simultaneously just wanting to feel his solidarity.

His strong arms encircle her, "Hey sweetling, everything ok?" Marcus isn't certain why but two things in his mind immediately connect. First, he knows that the evacuation of the hospital was not routine, and he now knows that Isadora is somehow connected to that. The fully armored police squad he saw at the end of Laurens hall as he was leaving the hospital flits across his mind. Something inherently protective and savage flares inside him.

"Yes, everything is great." The lie foul on her tongue. Looking up at Marcus she can see that he detects the untruth and she hates herself for it.

"No, everything is not great." Marcus presses. "We were just cleared to go back inside the hospital. Security said it was some sort of routine safety inspection. Isa, that isn't normal. I saw police officers decked out like some S.W.A.T extraction squad, going room to room. Is there some sort of dangerous prisoner ward here?" Marcus feels better at the look of shock on her face.

"Uh, no, not that I know of." The tension in Marcus's shoulders release, knowing that is the truth and wanting to respect her space he doesn't push further. He assumes her evasive behavior is due to professional privacy.

Officer Denis talks into his sleeve, "Yes Sir, they look intimately familiar. I will have his name ASAP."

"Come on beautiful, I will walk you in. I was looking for you earlier but the administrative secretary said you weren't in yet.

She said you were running late." Marcus hugs her to his side, concerned.

"Oh yeah, I had some car trouble, had to get a ride to work." Isadora grimaces again, feeling less guilty as that wasn't exactly a lie, *it was mostly the truth*, she reasons.

"I guess I feel a little stupid," Marcus chats happily, "I would have had the pleasure if we had exchanged numbers last night." He hands her his phone, allowing her to type the number herself. She smiles at the openness this simple gesture shows. She hands it back to him and he takes a quick picture of her without warning. "Now when I wake up in the morning I will have proof." Marcus kisses her forehead, amazed at his own ease of affection with her.

Isadora halfheartedly pushes him as she fusses over her hair, and simple cotton sundress wondering how disheveled she must look after her exhausting morning. "Don't feel bad, I had a… friend… pick me up." She hadn't meant to grind her teeth when she had exchanged the word for Officer Denis in her sentence, she hopes Marcus hadn't noticed. He had.

"Hey, is everything ok? You seem a little… stressed." Marcus asks her, noting an expression that looks like apprehension.

"Yes, I am fine. I probably won't be able to see you tonight, some … family stuff has come up." She looks nervously around for Officer Denis, hoping he is nowhere to be seen. She locates him in his unmarked car under a tree on the far side of the parking lot. Her face falls as she looks up to see that Marcus's gaze had followed hers. He is taking in what looks from this distance to be just some good looking fair haired military man. She watches as his brows furrow, praying internally that he doesn't ask. She wouldn't really know how to explain him to Marcus.

She needs to talk to Agent Maizer, the agent assigned to her case. "Um, Marcus, I was late and I have a lot to do today, can I call you later?" She blunders distractedly." Marcus's frown deepens, still looking at Officer Denis, he thinks, *she gave me her number, I didn't give her mine yet*.

She reaches on tip-toe kissing him quickly before she rushes inside. Leaving Marcus on the sidewalk pondering what exactly had just happened.

-25-
Not at all

"So, then she just rushed in the building and that was it." Marcus is explaining his meeting with Isadora to Luis.

"Maybe the fella in the car was an ex-boyfriend and he wasn't supposed to be around. You never know what has happened in someone's life before you came into it son. Your lady doesn't seem like a devious girl, just wait and ask her." Luis advises.

"Of course you are right Grandpa. I should just ask her. It did feel a little unworthy to be jealous. I'm not used to that at all."

"I understand, believe you, me. It was like that with my Janie at times."

"I'm sure it did with all that time away from each other, I can't even imagine what you thought could be going on." Marcus remarked, still pacing in an unsettled manner.

"Yes son, I would be lying if I said I never thought some rich kid with a fancy job and a fancier car may have come along and attempted to steal your grandmother away before I had a chance to really make her mine. But I always referred back to the moments on the bench in the church and in the cafe and *knew* that she was not a fickle girl that would give away her heart easily. I believed in who she was and her strength and passionate nature. I *had* too. You understand don't you son?" Luis asks when he looks up into Marcus's skeptical face.

Luis continues when Marcus doesn't confirm his understanding. "Love isn't doubting every second you aren't together. That is infatuation and insecurity. *Love* is the unintentional desire to believe the best in someone. It isn't a conscious effort, you just *do* believe in them and who they are. Their will and their integrity. Sometimes love is even stronger than what they believe of themselves. In fact, I know your grandmother always thought better of me and believed in me more than I believed in me and now I see I always did the same for her." Luis's face seems to shed years of age as his face brightens with his new found epiphany.

"I would say to you now Marcus that *that* is the part of being loved that makes us better people. When someone loves us like that we just *want* to be that amazing person in their eyes. When you are that deeply believed in you want to be the person they see you to be. You just want to live up to it, earn it if you will." Luis smacks the palm of his brittle dry hand on his pant leg producing a sound much like the collapse of a paper bag.

Luis stands, tottering slightly as he gains his footing. "I need to walk before I petrify. These old muscles threaten to become one with my bones every day." Marcus chuckles empathizing with the feeling but looking at Luis he doesn't see frailty, he sees vitality for a man near ninety.

"Ok, back to Laurens room or outside in the courtyard again?" Marcus inquires.

"I need to stay near a bathroom, too much coffee, what do you say we meander the halls?" Luis is hoping they will run into Isadora. He too is curious to see her behavior.

"Alright, so we were at the part where you had to return home from New York without grandma." Marcus assists.

"Ah, yes, I remember now, you had asked if Janie and I ever spoke of what happened to her when her father kept her from the bus station." Luis inhales deeply, swelling his chest with air as orators in Greece must have done in preparation for prolific narrations. "Well, of course we talked about it, so I will tell you her story as she told it to me and I will tell you what was going on with me as well. Try to keep up you." Luis teases.

Marcus smiles fondly yet remains silent. He is mentally welcoming the distraction from Isadora and his anxious feelings about her demeanor.

"Janie said that her father had made some connections with some unsavory men in New York. She told me that Ailfrid had gone from a grocer in California to owning a meat packing company in New York. Meat packing companies in New York and New Jersey do well whether they want to or not and part of that has to do with special services that unsavory families requested of them from time to time. Also being catholic didn't hurt him either since most of those families were catholic as well."

"Alifrid had, up to that night, been able to remain free of such an agreement because of his close relationship with the Mon Senior of the church. All of the best, which is to say the worst families went to church together and they had an unwritten code about what business was and was not conducted near and in the church. It is all exceptionally shady and corrupt otherwise, but in the church it was sacred and they were very devout, it was where they brought their families and wives, it was sacrosanct."

"At any rate when Ailfrid was plotting to take Janie again he needed to ask one of those families for help with her removal as he couldn't do it alone. He knew she was going to fight this time and he didn't have the heart to do the deed alone. It was shiftily done but in the end it worked out best for me and Janie because if her father hadn't been in the meat packing industry then I may never have found her again." Luis is striding purposefully down one of the many long corridors like a train engine working up steam. Marcus who is usually struggling to slow, is keeping a comfortable pace alongside him.

"So Janie was hauled off by Ailfrid's new unsavory friends and put on a boat." Marcus raises his eyebrows in surprise, noticing Luis plugs on, "Yes well I was surprised by that as well. Turns out Ailfrid had her shipped off to Italy that very same night." Marcus reels in shock.

"He really went that far? This is kind of crazy grandpa. Could he really want her away from you so bad that he would send her out of the country where he and his wife wouldn't see her either? It just seems kind of extreme if you ask me." Marcus interjects incredulously.

Luis raises an eyebrow and continues seamlessly. "As I was traveling across the country by bus, she was traveling across an ocean by boat and boy she never let me forget that while I was moping and feeling sorry for myself she was vomiting for weeks on end. I shouldn't have expected sympathy from her, she always gave me too hard of a time and I loved her for it." Luis smiles ruefully at the recollection. "That is when she began to write letters to me that became her journals that she continued to write until she died. At first she was writing letters and putting them in bottles hoping she would be able to throw them in the ocean. She admitted to that being a very silly and childish hope, but the men responsible for her found them and destroyed them. After that she was only allowed to have books until an old cook started bringing her empty journals and told her not to write anymore letters to me but to write to God and he would answer her prayers."

"Janie compromised by writing to me, not letters but of her thoughts and her feelings. Sometimes just a list of what she did for the day. She wasn't being treated like a prisoner, she was allowed to walk around the ship, it was a cargo ship, nothing pretty or fancy and she was given very plain clothes, nothing as beautiful as she was used to. She wrote of how free she felt in her captivity in some ways, that she felt no pressure or anxiety to live up to her father's domineering expectations and for the first time in her life she didn't have to fight with him daily to be heard and be accepted. He wasn't there to try and hammer her into his square hole, as she often put it."

"She wrote of the good days when she felt like a butterfly with wet wings getting the chance to stretch them and strengthen, and on the bad days where she felt like she was that same butterfly being dipped in the fathomless deep without hope of drying."

"I know this may sound strange to you and I never expressed it this way to Janie, but I think that trip was wonderful for her. To be so completely alone and without any strain other than basic needs. She was able to focus on her heart, her perspective and what she wanted to do with her life. She had no distractions, just alone with her thoughts."

"She said that when she finally got to Italy she was a woman, no longer a girl and her father would never have allowed that if she had stayed in New York with her parents. She thought that if she stayed with her parents she would have always felt guilty for growing up with her own wants and needs. As an only child she felt responsible for their happiness as much as her own. She had always been stunted in the natural progression of her life by trying to be what they wanted for her. She said once that she felt like she was a bad daughter to want a different life for herself, to want adventure and to educate herself in things that her parents deemed worthless."

"When Ailfrid put her on that boat he freed her of all that obligation and guilt." Luis sighs heavily, shaking his head. "It would have been such a waste for her to not become who she was when we were together. She touched so many people Marcus. She was an incredible English professor. She inspired her students to grow her favorite quote was, "Arrange whatever pieces come your way." By Virginia Woolf. She loved to encourage people to live, to take hold of life and really live."

Luis has slowed but is striding along easily, no longer stiff, shaking himself from the past back into the present, he shimmies awkwardly.

"I, on the other hand was miserable. I had no such freeing feeling from repression. I felt like I had signed over my life to toil away in angst." Luis looks up with an ironic smile. "Yes I was being melodramatic. I had everything I wanted and had it ripped away from me and now Uncle Sam was the one keeping me from finding my happiness." Luis chuckles.

"I was pouting, Marcus, and I kept pouting for months." Marcus chuckles with his grandfather. "There wasn't really much else I could do until I saved up more leave. I still had two years left on my enlistment and I had honestly planned on re-enlisting when that term had ended, that is until Janie happened to me again and the short time we had in New York we discussed her enlisting as well. She wanted to fly planes. Which back then was just not going to happen but Janie wouldn't hear of it. She said she would find a way to become a fighter pilot and she might have if her father hadn't intervened. I am telling you Marcus, your grandmother was some lady." Marcus nods in agreement, thinking she must have been.

Marcus contemplates the new information his grandfather is sharing with a seriousness he is unaccustomed to. Uncertain as to why it matters so much now, when it was all just a fun story two days before. "So, I'm sure that grandma had quite an experience in Italy but how is it that you two didn't find each other right away? Why didn't she write to you in California?" Marcus feels the unfairness of the situation much more deeply than he expected to. "I mean, directly… why didn't she just find a way to send you a letter at home?"

"Well, because as young and naive as we were, we had so much faith in love and our connection that we made a serious oversight. Can you believe that I never gave her my address or my unit information for the company and battalion I was in?" Luis chuckles as he shakes his head in apparent disbelief. "I tell you I just didn't think of it son, it was so, well, stupid. When I had found her in New York I was so dead certain that we were finally together that it never entered my mind to create a contingency plan in case we were ever separated again." Luis tisks loudly in self-admonishment.

Marcus stares in wide eyed silent shock.

"Yes, I know, don't look at me like that kiddo, I did mention it was stupid. The result of that lack of planning is that your grandmother and I kept very strict track of each other for many years after we finally got married. I think that fear of losing each other again made us closer than most couples. I have said it a hundred times if I have said it once. To realize love is when you become aware of how scared you are to lose someone. I lived it several times son, I *know* that statement to be solid fact." Luis pokes Marcus in the chest with his twisted, stick like finger, to drive home his point. Marcus smiles at the familiar gesture.

Luis and Marcus round a corner as Marcus rubs the slightly sore spot on his chest realizing that they have wondered through the halls back to the cafeteria and is astonished by the clatter and droves of people in the lunch room, indicating it is lunch time already. "Are you hungry grandpa?" Marcus asks hoping he may get a glimpse of Isadora while they dine.

"Oh sure, I could eat." Luis states as they enter into the candescent light of the bay windows in the large, busy room.

Allowing for a small break, both men remain comfortably quiet. Marcus scans the room for Isadora but does not see her. He remembers that she had said the cafeteria wasn't her main work area but had hoped for the sake of hoping, that he would run into her. "No such luck." He grumbles under his breath after searching the room for the fourth time.

Looking at the clock Marcus notes that it took them nearly forty minutes to get seated. "I had no idea it got this busy in here." Marcus makes small talk absently in Luis's general direction.

-26-
Please Don't

"Bothering you isn't it?" Luis cuts directly to the topic hanging in the air. Marcus considers feigning ignorance out of pride but is too agitated too prolong the anxiety.

"Yes. That obvious?" He looks into Luis's deep dark eyes, hoping for some sort of reassurance from the older man.

"Yes sir, it is son." Luis states flatly and takes an over large bite of his Ruben sandwich. Marcus shakes his head and scans the room again. In the far right corner of his field of vision he catches a glimpse of fabric. It is the dress Isadora was wearing that morning, swinging in front of one of the bay windows that is the view of the hall and further out into the courtyard. She is standing behind the solid part of the wall out of sight but her skirt peeks at him as she moves in what must be soft conversational gestures. Excitement rises in his chest and threatens to burst out of his throat. He swallows quickly.

"Keep your britches on kid, I see her, she is on the other side of that wall, she can't see you. Eat your food like a good boy and be still."

Marcus glares daggers at Luis for his condescending tone but can't maintain his anger as Luis winks at him in mirth. Luis's mouth is full to bursting and Marcus suspects Luis is stuffing his mouth to keep from laughing, he continues to glare as he finishes his own sandwich.

After they clear their trays, they exit together. Marcus looks down the long hall to where Isadora would have been standing. Spotting her he is alarmed by the worried expression on her face and the unknown words being exchanged between Isadora, the military guy from the parking lot and some other stuffy guy in a suit, Marcus takes a step towards them when a steel like clamp attaches to his arm. Luis has an unbelievably, strong hold on Marcus's forearm. Marcus pauses, long enough to register his grandfather's words, through his haze of concern.

"Don't go down there son, something isn't right. Something is going on that you don't understand. See that coil of clear tubing in the suit's ear? He is something other than just a cop son. Trust me, I have seen things." Marcus looks hard in the direction of the conversing trio, Luis is right, something is off.

Isadora is the only one facing him, the two large men have their backs to him. One of them steps to the side and Isadora looks between them through the gap. She and Marcus make electric eye contact and she shakes her head nearly imperceptibly to the negative. With a look of pleading in her eyes, she is telling him "No. Don't come to me. Please"

Luis speaks softly. "Come along Marcus." Startled by the use of his name he numbly follows the pressure of Luis's hand on his arm, pulling him away from Isadora.

Somewhat in a daze, Marcus shuffles down the hall in the direction of Lauren's room. "I can't say I'm not a little concerned grandpa."

"Yes son, I can see it is minimal." Luis teases, hoping to distract Marcus.

Marcus frowns, unsure of how to proceed. What seemed so simple and easy yesterday is now clouded with complications. When Marcus was in Isadora's sphere of happiness last night he felt certain and without doubt about how he felt about her and towards her. "But… Now I have so many questions grandpa, not doubts really, I know how I feel, but what will it mean? What *can* they mean? We live in different states. We have lives, lives that I am pretty sure neither of us could just walk away from. What if Lauren gets better and I leave and I never see her again?" As Marcus voices his random thoughts he acknowledges a profound, questionless security. "It doesn't really matter does it?" Marcus inquires of Luis, still hazy but reaching clarity quickly.

"No son, it doesn't. Nothing matters but what you want in life and out of life. If you need her in your life to get what you want out of life… Well, then you have your answer, just as I did. You do what you have to do and the whole rest of the world and what goes on in it have nothing to do with the hindrance or progression of your future with that girl."

"Come now, let's go check on your sister and see what they have decided to do with her." Both men turn simultaneously in the direction of Lauren's room. Silently contemplating the morning's developments.

Marcus looks down the hall one last time as they round the corner. Thinking of nothing but protecting Isadora. Finding out what is wrong and doing whatever he can to shelter her and help her return to the laughing, happy girl she had been the night before. *"What could have happened in the last sixteen hours?"* he wonders uselessly inside his head, picturing the armed officers form earlier that morning.

-27-
The Facts

"Lauren will be released the following Monday, we are keeping her here for observation as her kidneys are still a concern. All of the antibiotics we had her on to fight the infection have caused damage of their own and her body needs time to recover, the dialysis has helped. She is safe now, but not strong enough to go home. She is very lucky to have such a loving, supportive family. Having you here makes all the difference in my opinion. It must have. No one expected her to come out of this, if I believed in miracles..." The Doctor trails off as he scans the room for questions before taking Kevin's arm and leading him to the hallway.

Marcus scans the room as well looking at the joy and relief on the many faces that have become so familiar and his heart swells with affection for each of them. Settling on Jeff's face, the doe brown eyes of his nephew lift and meet his stare. Jeff rushes to Marcus and hugs him around the waist tightly. Murmuring into Marcus's stomach. "Thank you Uncle Marcus. I love you." Marcus's eyes finally react to the tension that the rest of his body has been feeling for days. Tears well in his eyes and trickle down his cheek to drip like spent diamonds on the top of Jeff's impossibly thick mop of brown spikes.

His tears are release of the strain and worry that he had been stifling in regards to Jeff's well-being and the unfairness of possibly losing his sister, while mingling with regret that he will no longer have a viable excuse to stay with Isadora. He has only two more days with her. It all seemed so exciting, hopeful and tragic. Marcus isn't accustomed to this kind of rollercoaster, and the tears seem a logical response to the sensory overload.

"Oh stop being such a baby, sheesh." Jeff's watery eyes look up into his uncle's face. Marcus's tears instantly disappear at the look of sheer joy and innocent hope emanating from the boy's face. Jeff's grin is infectious. Marcus grins widely in return. "Shut your face little man." He lifts Jeff and kisses him hard on the cheek, as he turns to the door to see where Kevin is.

Isadora is standing dejectedly, leaning against the wall directly across from Laurens hospital room. She raises her head guiltily and smiles weakly. Marcus wants so bad to go to her. She looks like she might have been crying or is scared. Marcus sets Jeff down with one last hug. Looking at Luis, he isn't sure for what reason, Luis mouths the word, "Gently." And looks away, making a small sweeping motion with one of his hands as though ushering Marcus from the room towards Isadora. Marcus nods. No one notices this exchange or Marcus leaving the room. Everyone is excitedly chatting with and around Lauren.

Unreasonably nervous to both tell Isadora the good/bad news of Laurens recovery and to receive Isadora's reason for coming to find him, he shoves his hands deep into the front pockets of his loose blue jeans and walks shyly to her side.

Posting himself with his back against the wall next to her, he looks up from the ground only to be assaulted with her piercingly intense gaze. He retreats into the nerdiest part of his mind imagining this is what it must feel like to be caught in a transporter beam on Star Trek. He looks back at the ground and smiles at his own idiocy.

"Good news huh?" She asking in a quiet almost defeated voice that breaks Marcus's shyness instantly turning it into protectiveness.

Without warning or invitation he wraps her up in his arms cocooning her from the world. She melds into his torso like a baby bird under its mother's wing. Feeling for the first time in her life like she doesn't have to be strong and in charge. She can trust Marcus to be those things for her.

"Whoa, I like this. This doesn't feel bossy at all sweetling." Marcus taunts gently. She burrows deeper as she laughs and hits him gently in the chest.

She doesn't remove herself so Marcus answers her question as a means to segue into their discussion of *what happens next*. "So yeah, it was good news. Lauren's doctors think she is going to make a full recovery. She will be going home next Monday."

Isadora does pull away beaming. "Yay, I am so happy for you and your family."

She looks it, Marcus thinks as her radiant joy erases any trace of the morning's unhappiness. *Wow, she really is selflessly happy for us right now.* He is moved by her transparently genuine concern. "Thank you, I appreciate that, it means a lot… but, you didn't come here to check on my sister did you?"

Isadora's face falls. Despair to match his own settles on her lovely exotic features and he notices how she places her hands behind her back and sways back and forth in a nervous gesture. In her sundress, with her contrite expression he can see her as a five year old little girl who just dropped her ice cream in the dirt and he melts. Every bit of hard, strong masculine male ferocity in him melts. Right into the floor at her feet. He has never felt so happily conflicted in his efforts to preserve his prowess before.

Reaching forward he removes her hands from around her back and hold them gently in his. "I know I play a lot sweetling but I am serious as all hell right now. You can't stand there like that or I will devour you right here in the hallway in front of my whole family." He looks at her guiltily, "And, I feel I should at least buy you several dinners and meet your family before I do that." He kisses her forehead. "When you look that desolate I don't know if I am supposed to cradle you or carry you off… OK?"

Isadora smiles weakly thinking, *I don't have any family.* "Ok Marcus, anything you say." She says it breathlessly and she can tell from the expression on his face that Marcus almost does carry her off. *God, this man makes me want to laugh even when I hate everything about the world,* Isadora considers.

She doesn't know what it is about *this* man that makes her such a powder puff. Something in the set of his strong jaw and how it matches the determination of will in his posture makes her want to become that soft girl that she has never been and hide behind him. She contemplates silently as she says aloud what she is thinking. "I trust you." Ripping her hand from his grip to cover her mouth in shock. She hadn't meant to say it out loud.

She had never said those words out loud to a man other than her brother Rodrigo. Long ago she found she wasn't able to put her trust in Rodrigo anymore either and she is astounded that she does indeed trust Marcus. She speaks her epiphany. "I will tell you everything." She knows that whatever Marcus's reaction is, she is safe with him. She pictures them on a couch in front of a fire with her head on his chest, content and secure for the first time in her life.

"Ms. Trevino? There is someone… uh… official here for you in the lobby." A candy striper interrupts her vision.

Marcus groans, Isadora rolls her eyes and pivots around facing the girl. All business again, she instantly sheds her weakness and heads in the direction of the lobby. Turning over her shoulder as she walks away. "Wait for me Marcus…" He can't hear the rest as her voice echoes in the sterile hall and the noise of the hospital returns to his consciousness.

Vowing to find her later that evening, he watches her round the corner disappearing from sight, he returns to Lauren's room.

-28-
Tomorrow

"Lauren wants to talk to you Marcus. Go on in and then meet me at the house. I am going to take the kids home. They already sedated her so she will be out soon." Kevin pats Marcus on the shoulder. He looks tired and he has lost weight, but relieved and more relaxed.

Marcus approaches Lauren's bedside slowly trying to stall for enough time to shrug off his worries and focus on her. Lauren reaches towards Marcus holding out her hand for him to take.

It strikes Marcus as an uncharacteristic gesture on her part, as Lauren had never been an affectionate sister.

Extending his hand tentatively, Marcus notices how paper-like her skin feels as he slides his hand into hers. Her entire body looks swollen to bursting. Her skin has the stretched look of a water balloon that had been filled to much in too short a time. Marcus is scared to touch her.

"Don't look at me like that." Lauren rasps. Her voice as frail and thin as her skin is taught. "I am still your big sister and I will kick your ass," She smiles then grimaces as though it hurts. Swallowing hard seems an exhausting effort for her.

"That happened one time… because for a very short time you were bigger and stronger than me." Marcus tries to sound nonchalant but feels as though he is failing epically. He knows it must show on his face or she wouldn't have said anything.

"My throat feels like I was in a coma and used harshly by men I don't know." Shocked and disgusted Marcus cringes, drawing a healthier smile from Lauren.

"Did you have a goal in mind for stressing that sorely worn throat or was your singular purpose to make me vomit?" He gags visibly for effect.

Lauren's weak smile flits across her tightly swollen lips. They look unnatural as does the rest of her body. Marcus is reminded unpleasantly of a gorged leach and his heart hurts for his formerly strong sister.

"I have been dreaming about you little brother. Since I woke up. You and a…" She points at the ice water pitcher on her bed tray. Marcus fills her cup and fits the bendable straw to her lips until she turns away.

Her voice is closer to normal after the water but still Marcus worries. "I feel like there is a lesson here, me being here…" Lifting her restrained IV hand slightly, she trails off as her eyes roll around the room slowly. "Weird isn't it; that I dream of you? You would think I'd be worried about the kids. But in my dreams…" Tears begin to trickle down her face and Marcus feels a sensation similar to twine twisting tight in his navel. "In my dreams, Dad has them and they are safe, I am safe because Daddy is there. You though, you are searching…" Marcus frowns, uncertain if she is talking about Kellan.

The puzzlement knits into the muscles of his face, he frowns at his sister but remains quiet. "Yes, Marcus, *your* father… *my* father. I have been so wrong all these years. I heard him talking to me when I was waking up, or asleep, or whatever." She shakes her head weakly trying to clear her thoughts. "I know he wouldn't be here if he didn't care. I know I love him too or I wouldn't make him my protector in my head. Tell him…" She is weakening again and her eyes flutter as Marcus feels pressure on his sleeve, turning he is face to face with their father.

Kellan had walked into the room to stand just behind Marcus as she had finished. Tears streaming down his face, Kellan sniffles, wiping roughly at the moisture beneath his eyes. Marcus is relieved that he will not have to convey that message to his father because he just wouldn't be able to do it justice.

Lauren's eyes open slightly as her eyes roll trying to remain conscious. Gripping Marcus's hand tighter but still alarmingly soft, Laurens eyes widen for emphasis as she speaks. "Fall in love Marcus, you are ready, let yourself fall in love." Her grip slackens and falls from Marcus's hand as she succumbs to the sedatives.

"Remind me to talk to her about Jeff when she is fully healthy. I have kept quiet for too long dad. Hopefully this will change Kevin's attitude, soften his heart a bit, but just in case, I have to say something."

Marcus looks at Kellan. Kellan raises his eyebrows. "If I wasn't so damn happy I would have something to say about what she just said, but since I am filled with nothing but joy and relief right now you are in the clear, in regards to you falling in love and speaking up about Jeff."

Kellan walks across the small hospital room to the window sill and looks out as he takes tissue from the flat box and blows his nose. "Maybe you should let me talk to Lauren about Jeff."

With his back still to Marcus and Lauren, Kellan asks, "I see you have been spending a lot of time with the old man. I can't say I'm not just a bit jealous. I thought you and I would get some Father/Son time before you have to head back to Vegas. Everything ok with him? His health? Any particular reason you have been stuck to him like fly paper?" Kellan turns as he finishes, targeting his son with a familiar parental stare.

Marcus almost laughs as a thousand memories flood his mind of times he had been the recipient of "the eyes" as he and Lauren had referred to the look Kellan wears now. Clearing his throat, "Eh Hem, you can put the eyes away dad. There is nothing I am keeping from you. Luis is in perfect health and I would tell you if he wasn't." Marcus states jovially.

"In fact, I think the old man could give us both a run for our money if we had to race him today." Marcus continues as Kellan chuckles knowingly. "We have just been doing a little bonding over his and grandma's love story. It is actually quite incredible. I want to make sure I get the rest out of him before I leave."

"Really? The old man has a story huh? Your mother used to hint at things about them but she never had much to say about them and when she did it was rarely good." Kellan says.

"Well, as I recall, mom rarely had anything nice to say… period. She never had anything nice to say about you to them either. Seems she was content to sew discord at every possible chance." Marcus thinks about Diane's confession about never loving Kellan and vows to never tell Kellan. Marcus is unwilling to let Diane soil their bond. *The best way to remove the power from hurtful words is to never repeat them, especially to the person they could hurt most.* Marcus thinks as he looks at his father, his heart filling with happiness and pride. *He is such a good hearted man. I am lucky he is my father.*

"Right you are, kid." Kellan shakes his head. "What do you say we go get some coffee on the way out? Didn't Kevin need you for something? We better get back to the house. Maybe help Kevin clean up, get things in order before your sister has to come home and nag him to death from her sick bed." Both men groan simultaneously in cohesive memory of Lauren's well known rants. "Good thing he loves her." Kellan says as they exit Lauren's room.

"Is it?" Marcus laughs teasingly.

As they walk by the cafeteria on the other side of the courtyard from Lauren's room, Marcus is reminded of Isadora. He looks in but does not see her. "Hey dad, you know how you always talked to me about what it feels like to be in love? Well, I think I might have met someone… at least someone who makes me think I can fall in love, when no one else has ever even made the topic enter my head, let alone my heart."

Kellan stops dead in the hallway. "You serious son or are you toying with your old man's heart? Are you talking about the girl that works here?" Kellan points at the cafeteria.

"Yeah, her name is Isadora. Ee-suh-door-uh," Marcus enunciates slowly, looking in his father's eyes for some indication of his mood.

"Well kiddo," He stuffs his hands into his pockets exactly like Marcus does when he is thinking hard, "She sure is a beauty. Is she good and kind? Smart? Funny?" He asks in quick succession like a BB gun firing.

"Yes, she is, all those things and more. But you know… it isn't even about all the things she is or isn't. It is about the things I feel when I am with her. I am so happy just to be alive and in her presence dad. It makes me want to make her smile as much as she makes me smile. It makes me think I can do anything. I feel energized and it isn't even remotely sexual… although…"

Kellan cuts him off. "Spare me the gore kid. You are still nine years old in my head. Besides a gentleman never tells. You had better be a gentleman or *I* will be kicking your ass. Your sister won't have too."

Marcus snickers like a child. "You heard her say that huh?"

Kellan laughs, "No, I missed that part, I just know Lauren. She brings that incident up every chance she gets. You will never get to live that down."

Marcus sighs heavily. Lauren had in fact given him a generous butt kicking when he was eleven years old. It was the last year that Lauren was bigger than he was and he never would have hurt her because his father had raised him to never hit women. However, the plain fact was, she gave it to him good for mouthing off and thinking he was big and bad. The end result being; he had a new respect for her after and didn't mouth off to her again.

Smiling at the memory while still being annoyed that she held the "girl card" from that point forward and being much bigger and stronger kept him at the disadvantage. He was never going to get a chance to put her in her place like she had done to him. To him that was the epitome of unfair but he had long since accepted it.

Now, in this moment, he would take another good butt beating and another lifetime of ribbing just to ensure that Lauren makes a complete recovery.

"So what about that coffee kid? Your treat?" Kellan punches Marcus in the arm.

After leaving a voicemail for Isadora, Marcus stops by the administrative secretary's office to leave a message for her, saying he will return at the end of her shift, just in case she needs a ride home or to pick up her car. Smiling thinking of the scent of her skin and the deep glints of russet orange in her eyes, he is looking forward to spending the next two days with her.

-29-
Now what?

The afternoon with Kevin and the kids passes quickly, filled with laughter and tickling. Watching Cassie and Kellan wrestle on the ground like a little girl and her pet monster is endlessly entertaining for all. Kellan being a big mountain of a man comparatively to his tiny granddaughter makes the antics of play all the more endearing. Jeff even ventures into the fray when Cassie calls for assistance. "Sabe me Jeffey, Sabe me…" She giggles uncontrollably as Jeff tries his best to remain dignified under the tickle assault.

After things calm and the kids settle in to watch a movie, the three men sit sipping an aged scotch that Kellan had bought Kevin for his and Lauren's wedding. It is dark, rich, smooth and exactly what they all needed. "This has aged perfectly Dad, I had never had a reason to open it until now. Lauren always asked me what I was waiting for… well, now we know. We were waiting for a miracle." Kevin sips, nodding his appreciation.

All three raise their glasses. "To Laurens stubborn nature." Kellan entreats.

In unison they all chime in, "To Lauren.

Several minutes pass before Marcus gets up suddenly with shoulders squared and set with purpose. "Gentlemen… I have to go." He begins gathering his keys and wallet. "I will be back later tonight. Isadora is about to get off work. I promised I would be there." Kellan and Marcus make meaningful yet silent eyes contact. Kellan nods his understanding. Marcus strides out the front door to his truck.

"Am I missing something? Who is Isadora?" Kevin asks.

"She is a girl at the Hospital. They met the first day Marcus got here."

"What? When? He has been with Luis constantly. When did he have time to hit on a girl?" Kevin laughs. "I guess when you look like a bronze God you don't have to hit on anyone. Good for him though, how many men can get numbers on his sister death bed? Not me that's for sure!" Both men laugh.

Kellan's face a mask of contemplation. *I suspect this one is much more than a dalliance.* "We will see." Kellan says both to himself and to Kevin.

Marcus arrives at the hospital in high spirits. The drive from Kevin's house to the hospital was one of building anticipation. He is aware that he and Isadora have some serious topics to discuss and that may be awful but all he could think the entire drive was, "I can't wait to see her face."

Barely putting his truck in park before he is catapulting himself from his truck, Marcus lands on the pavement in motion. Crossing the parking lot he is noticing how beautiful the evening is and how the sun is dropping lower in the sky. Looking at his watch, he is only seven minutes late. Isadora should have all of her things gathered and be ready to go.

Marcus's mood is soaring as he enters the lobby of the Hospital. It doesn't abate in the next twenty minutes he waits until he looks at his watch. It is nearing six when she should have gotten off at five. Remembering that he now has her number he decides to call her.

The first time it rings then goes to voicemail. He smiles hearing her seductive contralto voice requesting the caller leave a message. "Hey sweetling, I am in the lobby waiting. I thought you got off at five. Give me a call back when you get this. Oh, this is Marcus by the way. Talk to you soon."

Waiting a few more minutes, by exactly six Marcus is anxious. He walks to the administrative offices but they are closed for the night. Frowning he is confused. He doesn't even acknowledge the possibility that she isn't going to be there, he is just impatient and is itching to see her like a fiend going through detox.

Marcus sits down trying to quell his nervous energy. Concentrating on *not* concentrating on the time, Marcus pics up a TIME magazine, vaguely registering the article about the Columbian drug lords being hunted and captured by the FBI. Dismissively wondering about the police squad in the building that morning Marcus looks at his watch. The words "I will tell you everything." flit through his subconscious as he notices the tiny print beneath a split photo of tailored men, covering their faces with Brooks Brothers suit lapels as they leave a court house in New York. The captions states; Attorney David Aragon indicted in association with the Cali Cartel and a singular professional photo of the man named David that looks like it was cut from a business card. There is something familiar in the man's face that is prickling familiar. Marcus sets down the magazine, closing the article.

Marcus calls Isadora again. It goes directly to voicemail. Thinking maybe she was calling him when he was calling her he tries again. As the phone connects and it begins to ring, the tall militant man from the parking lot that morning exits the elevator.

Officer Denis had returned to the hospital to retrieve the personal affects that Isadora had left behind locked in her desk drawer, among them was her cellular phone. It rings audibly in his pocket as Marcus and he make eye contact.

Marcus had never seen or heard Isadora's phone but it was entirely too coincidental in his mind that this man's pocket was ringing simultaneously with Isadora's phone on the other end of his receiver. The ghost of a guilty expression and alarm crossed the man's face. This confirms for Marcus that the ring issuing from his pocket was from Isadora's phone. To test his theory he waits for the next ring and hangs up in the middle. The ring in the stranger's pocket ends.

Marcus stows his phone and locks eyes with the man. "Hello, Marcus." The man says plainly. This threw Marcus. He was expecting challenge or aggressive behavior of some sort from a man like this.

Forgetting his manners and not taking the time to work it out in his mind he asks bluntly. "How do you know my name? Who are you? Why do you have Isadora's phone?"

"I know your name because Ms. Trevino *(Marcus notices lack of personal investment)* told me who you are. Your other questions will remain unanswered. Suffice to say, I am not at liberty to speak to you about anything concerning Ms. Trevino or myself. Good night." Officer Denis attempts to walk by Marcus.

Marcus steps in front of him fully aware of the threat emanating from the other man. Assessing quickly that this man is corded with muscle if his neck is any indication of his fitness level and that everything about him says that he is familiar with hand to hand combat. Marcus had guessed soldier earlier and this continued estimation only furthers that line of thinking. *I might get my ass kicked here.*

Officer Denis stops, clearly annoyed, sighing deeply. "Please step aside?" He asks his deep voice grating on Marcus's nerves. Officer Denis steps to the side but Marcus grabs his arm, they pivot together as the taller man is thrown off balance. Ripping his arm from Marcus's grasp his jacket opens exposing his detective's badge. Marcus notices the glint of metal and releases the officer's arm before he asks. "Hey, sorry, I didn't know you were a cop." Marcus continues uncomfortably aware that he could be arrested for assaulting an officer. "I thought you were an ex-boyfriend or something."

"My name is Detective Denis. There is nothing I can do for you man. If she was my girl I would be concerned too. But if you touch me again I *will* arrest you, okay?" Denis straightens his jacket and turns to leave. Marcus nods, confusion drowning his brain.

As the automatic doors open Marcus calls after Detective Denis. "Hey, is she alright? She isn't hurt or anything is she?" He honestly doesn't know what else to ask he just doesn't want the man to leave.

Detective Denis turns and says matter-of-factly, with a slight hint of empathy, "She is unhurt, and you never saw me here." He strides into the night.

Marcus stands frozen for an unknown amount of time, trying to formulate all of his errant concerns into a viable process. His first clear thought comes from between his lips without intention. "Luis, I need to see my grandfather."

Marcus jogs to his truck and speeds down the freeway to Luis's hotel.

-30-
Just unfair

"I know it isn't what you wanted to hear and I know that you thought it was all over. We are sorry it has to be this way but you have to go back into witness protection until we can find out just how many of the cartel are still out there trying to get to you." Agent Maizer is placating Isadora and she is getting sullen instead of uplifted.

"You told me that my move to San Francisco would be the end of it. That I could start my life over, that my leaving would ensure my and Rodrigo's safety. You told me a million things that made me leave everything I knew. How do I know that I won't have to just change my life again and again? This is no way to live." An image of Marcus and the feel of kissing him crosses her mind, making tears well in her eyes.

"When I left Florida it was because you told me that they would use me against my brother and that he wouldn't testify if I wasn't safe. I was ok with that at the time because I didn't have family but Rodrigo and it was for him. I left everything I had ever known, every friend I had ever made. I grew up there and now, I am just beginning to feel normal and it starts over? This is all just so unfair. *I didn't do anything to deserve this.*" The last sentence nearly a yell.

Agent Maizer takes on a condescending tone, "Oh you think your brother deserved this? You think he asked to be sucked into an organization that would have potentially found him and killed him after they tortured you to death to get to him? Everything he did was to protect you. Now that he is gone are you…"

Isadora's temper flares. "Don't talk to me like I am a petulant child Agent. My education far exceeds your own, so my intellect is not lacking, my acceptance of your department's ineptitudes is where my understanding falters." Isadora stands up, pacing the cheap hotel room. "You don't even know for certain if the incident at my high rise this morning was related to me. This seems like a bit of an overreaction." Isadora pauses in her rant when she notices the look of hesitation on Agent Maizer's face.

"There is something you haven't told me." It isn't a question it is a statement. Isadora sits back down, her head in her hands.

Agent Maizer begins slowly, tentatively so as to avoid Isadora's anger. Anger he had never witnessed in the beautiful woman before. Something in her life had changed and she is now unwilling to lose it.

Agent Maizer recalls something his wife had said to him when he had first come out of Quantico and was working his first dangerous case. "I only yell and get angry when I have something worth fighting for." She had meant him and their marriage, so he now recognizes the sign of a woman hunkering down for a fight.

"Ms. Trevino, we have intelligence that family members of the cartel that we put away two years ago have surfaced. Family members that we as an agency had been unaware of. They had up to this point never been seen in person by any law enforcement. They hadn't ever been major players and had escaped our notice. Now with all of the old regime dead or imprisoned, they are either looking for revenge or to build a reputation." Agent Maizer scratches his five o'clock shadow, fidgeting.

"Two weeks ago one of our undercover agents was killed after delivering a message to a safe house. The message had flight plans for Half Moon Bay, a private airport south of San Francisco and pictures of these unknown family members and a scribbled note on the back of Rodrigo's indictment photo that had your name, both your old and new name." Agent Maizer pauses, "That Agent died to save *your* life Isadora. I'm not telling you this to make you feel guilty, I am telling you so that you understand the gravity of these people being in this city." He takes Isadora's hand in his as he sits on the coffee table in front of her. She looks up into his sincere face. "You are the only person of interest in San Francisco right now. The only person *they* would be interested in. They have to be looking for you. We don't know why. We just know that they are. Okay?"

Tears stream silently down Isadora's face as all the fight goes out of her. She nods understanding. Marcus's face looms behind her eyes when she closes them. The tears come steadily until she falls asleep curled in a ball on the horrible scratchy couch in a dank hotel room on a street of which she doesn't know the name.

Marcus is leaving Luis's hotel after having pounded on the old man's door for twenty minutes and several phone calls without result. Walking out through the reservation desk lobby, hands deep in his pockets, he passes the lounge where he had eaten with Luis and Alice.

"Hmm, couldn't hurt." Marcus mumbles under his breath as he decides to get some food. *Maybe they will come back while I eat.* Looking at his watch it isn't nearly as late as he thought.

As he enters the inviting room he hears a familiar chuckle. By now, he would know that chuckle anywhere. He is so relieved that he actually smiles for the first time in hours.

Wearing that smile, Marcus approaches the table, trying to keep his mood in check. "Mind if I crash the party?" Marcus asks. Ricky, Alice and Luis all smile beguilingly up at Marcus. It is obvious they are glad to see him and he is stunned by the change that Lauren's situation has brought to his family.

"Of course kid, have a seat. You're so good looking you will up our stock over here." Alice says, scanning the room with a caustic look of appraisal. Marcus wants to laugh but he just smiles. It seems he just doesn't have it in him to laugh with so much strain in his body. He seats himself in the horseshoe shaped booth as Alice slides in closer to Ricky.

The conversation continues on course but Marcus, unable to keep up as his mind keeps drifting to the events of the day. He can't seem to fit everything in place. He knows he doesn't have all the pieces of the puzzle and every time he tries to make sense of everything he feels like he has less and less information. He still had not heard back from Isadora. He is beginning to wonder if she is in real trouble and what it could be.

He remembers that the candy striper had said someone "official looking" was at the hospital for Isadora. At the time Marcus thought it had been something to do with hospital staffing but now he knows that makes no sense. The candy striper would have known a fellow employee. It must have been Detective Denis that had been there.

Legal issues just don't fit with the person he thought he knew Isadora to be. She isn't shady, she isn't guarded. She *is* highly educated, well-spoken and kind. People like that are usually not criminals. If she isn't a criminal, maybe she is a victim, Marcus thinks and the thought makes his stomach revolt.

He looks down at his half eaten plate of food. Incapable of remembering if he had ordered and when. "*Hey*...hello? Earth to Marcus. You ok kid?" Ricky asks, touching Marcus on the hand.

Startled, Marcus shakes his head, looking up to the expectant faces. They had obviously asked him a question and were waiting for an answer. "I'm sorry, what was that?"

"You ok? You aren't still worried about Lauren are you?" Luis asks.

"Uh, no! Lauren is doing well. We had a chance to talk. She said something about her dreams. Did you all get the chance to talk to her while you were in the room this morning?" They all nod in the affirmative.

"Yeah, I'm sorry I didn't get to talk to you guys myself, I just had something..."

Luis interrupts his disjointed thought with a laugh. "Oh we saw you with your girl. You two looked like the only two people in the world in that hall. Where is she now? Why are you here with us old codgers and not out convincing that girl to be the mother of your..." Luis stops at the stricken look on Marcus's face.

Marcus's expression so distressing that Alice put her gnarled hand on his, patting him as though comforting a child. "What's going on Marcus?" She asks, always straight to the point.

Marcus relays the conversation with Isadora, and the succeeding events with the detective, in detail. He is hoping they will offer some perspective he had yet to consider.

-31-
Endings

Luis opens the door of his hotel room entering slowly and warily. Luis is shaking his head as he shuffles. "Son, I have to say, I'm not sure what you should do or what you *can* do." Luis removes his light London Fog jacket and slings it over the back of an armchair, places his room key on the table and removes his shoes.

All of this is necessary and things that Marcus himself would have done upon entering a hotel room, but the way the clock has seemed to slow in function is grating on Marcus's frayed nerves.

It has been the toughest and most unstable day of his life. First, the news that Lauren is going to fine, the joy and relief involved had Marcus's heart soaring. Then to have that elation immediately followed by the plummeting sorrow of his distance and inability to get answers concerning Isadora has him feeling like he was riding a roller coaster of emotion. Marcus sits in the armchair holding Luis's Jacket.

"Let's look at this reasonably… All you have is her number and where she works. You know that detective now has her phone. You also know the police have her or at least have her safe. You don't know where she lives. You don't have any real information about this girl. It seems she is involved in some sort of crime that likely is exposing her to danger, because truthfully she doesn't seem the type to be party to it. You don't really have any options… any more than I did when Janie disappeared." Shaking his head with compassion Luis settles into the chair opposite Marcus.

"I don't envy what you are going through kid. I have been there, as well you know. It is painful." Luis reaches to pat Marcus on the knee comfortingly. "However, assuming that she isn't a hardened criminal, she now has your number and your messages… if the police are allowing her to have that phone back." Luis cringes as he comes to that conclusion aloud.

Marcus just looks at his grandfather, the storm of conflict clearly written on his face.

At a loss for how to comfort the younger man Luis looks around the room hoping to trigger some sort of helpful thought process.

Looking defeated Marcus asks, "How did you do it grandpa?" Luis shrugs unseen by Marcus as he was staring trancelike at the floor.

"Well, boy… we… Janie and I had just decided to not find anyone else. That is the true trick to lasting love you see?" Marcus shakes his head in misunderstanding.

"It is really just that easy Marcus. When you find someone that you want to be with more than anyone else, you close yourself. You close your eyes to the beauty of others, the laughter that makes you feel happy too, you close your heart and mind to the possibility of letting any other person in. Understand?" Luis leans from his seat to pat Marcus roughly, sharply, to make a point. "I am of the firm opinion that *that* is what is wrong with all the marriages that end today. There is so much excess and access to that excess. With computers, cell phones, social media, TV and publications. You never have to leave your home to find a thousand people to adore you. Why would anyone *work* at keeping one person's attention when they have so much attention and so many people who have access to them?" Luis finishes in a frustrated tone of voice.

Marcus is astounded at the older man's awareness of the world and technology. Most people Luis's age are stuck in their generation and have little interest in furthering their knowledge of the present. *Yet another admirable aspect to him.* Marcus reasons inside his head.

Luis continues after a long ragged breath of irritation, "I think it was actually easier for us in the 50's to love and be committed because there was less access to temptation. It seems like the invention of the TV was the beginning of all that temptation being brought into the home. It put sex appeal and variety right there in our faces. It used to be when I was young that we found someone we liked and that was enough for us because we just felt lucky to have a woman that wanted to walk side by side with us through life. We didn't have hundreds of gorgeous women running through our field of vision all day long. We had pin up girls sure, and like your grandmother, they were incredible works of art, lookers like you wouldn't believe. We just weren't flooded with images of what we *could have* like people are now. These celebrities and models are everywhere, constantly and they are perfected beyond the true spectrum of reality. They are so much in our homes now that I hear people talking about them like they know them. It is all so suffocating and sterile at the same time. I don't know if your grandmother and I would have made it if we were separated in this day and age. There is just too much!"

"Forgive me kid, I know you are hurting and what I am saying might make it all sound even less possible. I just see how young people your age and some even your father's age get distracted from what, at some point, really matters to them and it makes my old heart sore… Really loving is a decision more than a feeling…" Luis trails off sadness heavy in every word. "You have to decide to love, you have to let yourself and you have to open yourself up to letting them know you and love you, all the ugly, gritty parts of you. If you don't make that decision, you will always be open to everything and everyone else.

Looking up to his grandfather's face Marcus notices how some of Luis's vibrancy has faded with his sadness. Luis suddenly looks every bit his age as his face, shoulders and prowess sag under the weight of his thoughts.

"No worries," Marcus says perking up some for Luis's sake. "I need to stop feeling sorry for myself. Life isn't over. Is isn't like Isadora is in another country. Or stolen in the middle of the night. I just am not getting my way and I am pouting."

Marcus squares his shoulders, sitting up in his chair. "I have to go back to Vegas in a day and a half I have to at least try to find her. I am going to sit here and think about that. If Isadora hasn't called me back by this evening I will go down to the police station and find out how and where Detective Denis can be contacted. Also, you have to finish telling me about grandma before I have to leave." Marcus is the one to pat Luis this time.

"You know old guy… I appreciate you being here for me. I has occurred to me that you are one of the very few people in the world who can commiserate with me so specifically."

Luis laughs his gruff barking laugh. "Old guy indeed." Luis points to the plastic wrapped cups that housekeeping had left next to the ice bucket. "How about you go down the hall and fill up that bucket after you hand me those glasses?"

Marcus returns shortly to find Luis comfortably settled into the plush deck chairs on the mini patio of his room. On the end table between the deck chairs there is a bottle of Don Julio 1942. Marcus whistles in recognition of the beautiful tall, aquiline bottle of reserve tequila. It is holding down the basic training picture of Janie that Luis had shown Marcus that first day in the waiting room.

"You got out the good stuff huh?" Marcus gestures towards the bottle. Luis turns from the view to look at Marcus. A light breeze lifts the feather light, white tufts of hair behind Luis's ears. He looks strangely majestic in his linen shirt with the embroidery down the front. The white of the linen and the light blue of the embroidery somehow ad an elegance to the scene. Luis could easily be a wealthy Don relaxing on the veranda of his Spanish style, limestone home in Guadalajara. Marcus has a strange yearning to see that world, through the eyes of a wise old man who has known love, loss and the richness of family… and he wants to be that old man and he wants to see those things with Isadora.

"Sit down Marcus." Luis says seriously, handing Marcus two fingers of the aged tequila in the tumbler. Marcus sets the ice bucket on the table to take the glass. Relaxing into the deep cushion of the deck chair as Luis places the bottle in the ice.

Looking at Marcus seated next to him, in exactly the same extended cross leg position, an arm tucked behind his head. Luis settles back thinking, *we could be the same man in different spans of time if Marcus wasn't so much taller and more muscular.* Luis considers how he had been taken aback by their resemblance to each other when Marcus had walked into the waiting room three days ago. It was like his past-self had walked into his present to remind him of all the years that had passed by.

"She had made that decision same as I had," Luis begins, assuming that Marcus knew he was talking about Janie, "she was in Italy for over a year when she decided that she was going to take her life into her own hands. She had been a ward in a convent and they had been grooming her to become a nun. She had never agreed to become a nun but Ailfrid's friends had made generous contributions to that mission for years. Old Italian families have connections everywhere and prior to being sent to the convent she had been staying with an international lawyer and his family. One of the lawyer's sons had fallen in love with Janie and after months of being rebuffed, the father had her sent to the convent to get her out of sight and out of mind."

"Janie was never going to say vows. Not to anyone but me that is. She had a good relationship with God but she wasn't intended for that life. She was too dynamic, too alive, vivacious and adventurous."

"She had been doing good works at a local orphanage with the sisters when she saw a sign advertising a USO tour visiting the troops in three weeks. She began to plot to get to that show. She believed that she could get a job as a performer since she had been a Ziegfeld girl. The problem was that she needed to get her passport from the lawyer or the USO would never take her out of the country." Luis pauses to sip his tequila, Marcus follows suit.

"Wow that is smooth." Marcus sucks air in through his lips as though cooling his mouth.

Luis smiles with a raised eyebrow, an expression of sly knowing plays around his eyes. "I am old son, as you keep reminding me every time I look at you. If and when I drink, I only drink the good stuff." He winks. "Only you young fellas can drink that cheap rot-gut and live the next day to tell the tale." Both men laugh thinking of their past athletic exploits.

"After Janie saw that poster for the USO, she said it was like someone lit a fire in her heart. She began calling the son of the lawyer and found out that he was engaged to a girl and had forgotten about her. She talked him into sneaking her passport away from his father and giving it to her the night of the show."

"I don't know how she did it Marcus, but there was just something about Janie that made people believe her and believe in her. I think it was that she was just so earnest and passionate. She believed so deeply that it made you want to believe too. Her fervor was so genuine that it made you question why you would even question her faith… in whatever she was set on. It was both enamoring and endlessly frustrating. Try arguing with someone that believed in their rightness so diligently." Luis takes another sip smiling fondly, raising his glass in silent toast to a memory he isn't sharing.

"The night of the show Janie met with Aldo, the lawyer's son, he gave her the passport and some money to travel. It turns out Aldo had some conscience about the convent and what his family was doing to Janie. Since he was happy and getting married he wanted Janie to have a chance at the same."

"During the show Janie saw a girl she thought looked remarkably like a childhood friend. She wasn't certain since she hadn't see the girl for nearly fifteen years. She waited around and it turned out that the stunning red head she had known as a girl had become a stunning woman. Her friend, Florence took her to the director… well to make a long, long story a little shorter… Janie got her wish to be in the USO."

When she told me this part of our story it seemed almost like a modern fairytale. I told her often that she should write a book about her life. The USO is where she stumbled into modeling. Before that she had only done professional photos for the Ziegfeld show. She was a pinup girl as you may know. Nothing questionable or revealing, she just had the perfect look. Have you ever seen the pictures? She was my own Snow White. Raven hair and lips red as a rose just as the story goes."

Marcus can tell that the alcohol is taking effect. The more Luis speaks, the slower and more relaxed his speech becomes. A hint of his accent tinges the R's in his words. Marcus smiles wondering what Luis had sounded like as a young man. Marcus wonders if his deep voice and Latin accent had been one of the appeals for his grandmother. A scene from Never Talk to Strangers makes Marcus recall a swaggering Antonio Banderas all smooth charm and dangerous sexuality. Marcus shakes his head, never picturing Luis as dangerous in that way, more just dangerous to the heart of a young girl.

Marcus feels the heat of the Tequila as well, looking down at the empty glass in his hand. He is feeling a little light, warm and knows his imagination is getting the better of him. Thinking of Isadora he looks at his phone. There are no missed calls. It is late in the evening now, and he had hoped that Isadora would have cleared up her issues with the police by now. He is disappointed. He is frustrated. He is tired. Yet, he remains hopeful.

The sound of ice shifting in the plastic bucket brings Marcus out of his head, back into reality. Marcus watches as Luis pours the second drink, another two fingers of tequila. Marcus looks at the elegant bottle as Luis tilts it towards Marcus, asking silently if he would like another drink. Marcus holds out his hand for the bottle.

As he pours himself a drink Luis continues. "Have you…Seen the pictures of Janie when she was young?"

Marcus replaces the bottle back in the bucket. "Yes, I saw many of them when I was a little boy. I don't remember exactly why mom was packing or unpacking them or even where we were. I just remember sitting in the bottom of a closet with mom and her showing me a bunch of frames with old black and white photos." Marcus sips his drink. "She was really beautiful grandpa."

"Yes she was." Luis whispers.

Marcus leans back in his chair, checking his phone again. Nothing.

Luis notices the movement. "She would have called if she could son. Your connection is true. Believe in it. Believe in what you saw in her eyes. How she made you feel. Make the decision Marcus. What you believe is what is real. Not what your doubt tells you. Not what your loneliness and the unfairness tells you. Those things are only real if you believe in *those things*. Believe in your heart that you will find her and it will be so." Luis finishes with purpose in his voice. "Just like Janie did. That is how she came back to me."

Marcus's neck almost kinks as his head swivels to look at Luis in surprise. "I thought…"

Luis interrupts him. "Yes, I know, everyone in the family talks about how I found her, I went looking for her after she was spirited away from California..." Luis's accent is getting thicker as the tequila disappears from his glass. Marcus listens to the lilt in his voice. "The fact is, no one has ever asked me to go into detail for them so no one knows what really happened. You asked and have listened nicely, so I am happy to tell the story and share my tequila with my grandson."

"Well thank you. The tequila is great, as is the story. It is definitely helping to keep my mind off of Isadora." Marcus looks over at Luis. His eyes are closed and he is very still.

"Hey, you aren't getting out of this now, no sleep for you, you have to finish the story."

Luis opens one eye and glares at Marcus. "Selfish kid. I am an old man. I need my rest." He states with way to much energy to be convincing. "Now that Lauren is doing better I won't feel the least bit guilty sleeping in." Draining his glass in one swallow he sets the glass on the table a little unsteadily.

-32-
Running

"So you are telling me that I can't call him back and that I *have* to leave right now? Start all over again?" Isadora rages at Agent Maizer.

"You just met this guy Ms. Trevino. Is he really worth dying for? Are you really *that lonely?*" Isadora opens her mouth to rebuke the rude remark but Maizer continues. "We have only one of them in custody. Four of them flew into the city to come for you. We caught their flight by accident. I can't express to you enough that the *only* way to protect you is to relocate you." Maizer is getting upset now as well, Isadora can see the veins sticking out in his forehead as he pounds on the table.

Detective Denis and the Police Chief stand quietly in the corner of the room by the door. They look bored and annoyed as though they are missing out on some family engagement. *My life isn't boring you robots. I wish it were.* Isadora thinks as she makes defiant eye contact with Denis. He shrugs and looks away.

Maizer rants on, "If you don't do this, you could be killed. That boy you met, Marcus. They will kill him too. You know that don't you? In case you have forgotten… four years ago they almost killed your brother before he could testify. He bled out internally on the stand after being shot six times under our care… in protective custody! He did that instead of recovering completely in a hospital to put all those drug lords away. He was in a coma for seven months after only to die for his trouble. The last thing he said was, "Tell Nina she should be safe now and I am sorry." Isadora winces at the sound of the name her parents gave her.

Tears run down her face at the memory of what her brother went through. He had been the only person she had left after their parents worked themselves to death. They had grown up hard and Rodrigo had struggled to get his law degree and make a life for them. He was putting her through medical school when he got caught up with the Columbians.

Now the Columbians are depriving her of a normal life still. She was going to have to give up Marcus to keep him safe and away from her past, her brother's past. A past that really had nothing to do with her other than her being related to a man they needed to launder money for them. *God I hate them.* She screams inside her head. *It just isn't fair… but life has never been fair, I have always known.*

Isadora stands up and begins to pace. "I want my phone. I just want to say goodbye. Marcus doesn't deserve to feel rejected and abandoned. He shouldn't be hurt by this too."

Detective Denis removes the phone from his pocket and hands it to her. Both the Chief and Maizer try to stop him but he holds up his hand and speaks. "The service isn't on anymore remember? We had it turned off. Maybe she wants some voicemails or notes that she saved in it. She can't call out or email."

The agent and the chief relax. Detective Denis turns his back to them and makes eye contact with Isadora. He blinks down at the phone and back up to her face then back at the phone and frowns inclining his head towards it, before he walks back to his place on the wall. Isadora recognizes that he is trying to secretly indicate something to her but she doesn't know what it is. She begins to think hard about what he said. *"Voicemails or notes that she saved."* That's right she could take pictures and save notes on her phone.

Isadora sits down quietly hugging herself tight.

"We need your permission Ms. Trevino. We need you to sign consent forms. We do realize how difficult this is. We just want to keep you safe. At least until we catch these guys." Agent Maizer sounds tired and irritated. "These drug lord families… we think we got them all and then years later they come crawling out of the woodwork like cockroaches." Maizer runs his hands through his hair. He looks a mess. His usually polished shoes and stiff suit are scuffed and wrinkled as though he hadn't slept in days.

Isadora concedes. "Ok, bring me the paperwork. I will do this all again, but I want to leave tonight. I don't want to spend another day in San Francisco." *I can't be this close to him and know I will never see him again. I have to get away or I will go to him.*

She stands up again, walking towards the double doors that separate this main part of the suite from the bedroom.

"Where are you going?" Maizer asks.

"To the bathroom. May I pee? Or do I need an escort for that as well? I don't believe there are any windows in there." She pushes past the three men leaving them speechless.

-33-
Decisions

"Janie toured with the USO for their last ten shows before returning to the States. She had a modeling career and her pin-up ad where she is dressed in a mechanics jumpsuit, black petrol smudged on her perfectly alabaster skin and red kerchief on her head. It was doing very well. I of course hadn't seen it yet as it was released overseas but her future looked bright. She had no reason to come looking for me."

"In fact the day she came back home, she called her old boss from The Follies show and he offered her an audition for some new show he was doing. She was nervous about contacting anyone in New York because her parents and her father's Italian acquaintances were all there waiting for her to show up. Aldo had confessed to his father what he had done once Janie left Italy and Ailfrid and his pals had already hunted down my friend Joe and tried to get information out of him. Which of course they couldn't do. He didn't know anything."

"Janie had suspected that her father would have taken such precautions so she avoided New York all together, insisting on meeting her old boss in Palm Beach where he lived when not producing in New York."

"Unfortunately for Joe and for me, the Italian mob guys in New York had put a tail on Joe and his wife in case they tried to contact me. They were even filtering Joe's mail, hoping to intercept any correspondence between us. He didn't dare contact me or they would have burned down his butcher shop, literally."

"They needn't have bothered. Your grandmother was too smart for all that. They thought she was poor and alone and without options. They didn't know she was with the USO as Aldo had the good sense to omit having met her at the show to give her the passport. It was all very dime store novel stuff the way Janie told it, and I was none the wiser. Still enlisted, depressed and having thrown myself into my duties as a result, I was moving up through the ranks quickly and getting my education at night."

"By the time Janie was sitting at dinner with her former producer in Florida, I was stationed at Ft. Benning, Georgia. We were so close to each other and we didn't even know. Janie and I used to sit and talk for hours about little coincidences like that. She used to always say, "It was meant to be, God kept giving us chances and bringing us closer and closer together." And she was right."

"While I was running up the hills of hell at airborne training at Ft. Benning, she was being wined and dined by her old boss. In fact, he had designs on my Janie that were not honorable in the least. She told me that he had made passes at her and tried to kiss her after the long dinner. The evening went so badly that she slapped him, broke a heel and had to limp back to her hotel where she saw a bus stop ad to enlist in the Army."

"She told me how she thought about it all night and took it as a sign that she saw that ad right in front of her hotel on the way home from that type of evening and swore that she hadn't noticed that ad at all when she was getting into the limo to go to dinner or the three times she had come and gone from the hotel that day. My Janie believed in signs, both literally and figuratively. She stayed up most of the night thinking about what she was going to do and woke up the next day with a clear answer." Luis dips his glass into the ice bucket and fishes out some ice to suck on while he talks.

"You know she went down and enlisted in the Army that day. She used to tell me the funniest stories about basic training and how she had to make a huge fuss to become a B1 bomber mechanic. By the time she got out of basic her pin-up ad had hit the United States. There were billboards across the country with your grandmother's gorgeous face supporting the claim that Lava Soap could remove anything from your skin from 1893 until present."

Luis laughs heartily, "You know your grandfather was an idiot boy back then and even though my girl's face was everywhere, you know I never saw any of those dang billboards? Most men in the country saw her face before I did."

"Six months after Paratrooper training I was sitting in a chow hall in Ft. Huachuca, Arizona listening to a bunch of G.I's talk about the model who was supposed to have transferred to base that morning. I of course wasn't the least bit interested in some stupid model dame. I couldn't have cared any less if her hair was on fire. I was still pining after your grandmother."

Marcus is on the edge of his seat now, thinking he knew where Luis was heading with the story, but not wanting to miss a thing.

"I honestly got so sick of hearing about this girl I wanted to hire someone to get rid of her. I had to hear about her long legs in the chow line and her waist length hair in the showers. I had to hear about how they think she was sleeping with the Post General to get her uniform fitted so perfectly. I heard about the color of her lipstick and how great she looked climbing up and down those ladders to the plane engines. It was getting excessively nauseating to hear about this sensational female day in and day out. I swear I hated that girl and I had never seen her face. I just was sick unto death of listening to the guys fawn over her. Four months later I still hadn't seen her because I was a grunt and our barracks were on the opposite side of the post from the airfield. Not that several of my buddies hadn't tried to show me photos and ads, they had, I just refused to get on the band wagon. The way I saw it… she had plenty enough admiration and attention without adding me to the bunch."

Marcus laughs knowingly, thinking of the cheerleaders in high school and the volleyball players in college.

"Besides, no girl could have held a candle to my Janie and by that time, I don't mind admitting, *in my head*, Janie had reached immortal goddess like status." Luis throws a piece of ice at Marcus playfully. "That's what happens you know? When you lose someone you thought was amazing and beautiful without ever having known them well enough to know their flaws… they just get more and more perfect in your mind. It's a bit crazy really but it is human natu…" Luis trails of realizing what he is saying and how it will soon apply to Marcus. "I am sorry son. I hadn't meant to say that. I didn't think, I was caught up in the story."

"It's ok," Marcus says, the excitement leaking out of his smile like the ice had leaked down Luis's shirt. "I didn't think of it like that. I had forgotten for a moment about my situation. Please continue."

Luis begins again more sober than before. "Well, there I was sitting next to Red, one of the most annoying guys in my unit, again listening to him harp on about some dame he had met in town, as he was always meeting some unfortunate girl and regaling us all with tall tale of his exploits with women. I think he was probably a virgin because he was carrot topped and his freckles were set so close together and simultaneously, so far apart, that he looked like an unfinished paint by numbers kit." Marcus chokes on a harsh laugh.

"That's funny grandpa, I know just what you mean. We had a guy on the team with inconsistent freckling that we called spotty… his name was Scotty, but you know how it is with the guys?" Marcus laughs again.

"Indeed I do son. So Red is sitting there lying to our faces about some dancehall girl when in walks this tall raven haired girl with her hair braided and twisted up in two buns at the nape of her neck. I am telling you, I have never seen overalls look so good. I had to stare at my plate out of shame and guilt. I felt like I was cheating on Janie even though it had been a good long while since I had seen her. I even tried to tell myself that is the reason I was fighting myself over this girl."

"I was sitting there with my face in my tray telling myself that I only liked what I saw because of her similarities to Janie. Also noting the differences. My Janie was slighter of frame. Her shoulders weren't as wide and her waist was narrower. Her backside wasn't that round and full… so on and so forth until I convinced myself that Janie was in every way better than this girl even though I hadn't yet seen her face to truly compare. I ate my whole meal like that. My neck hurt."

"Oh, so that wasn't grandma then? I thought for sure you were going to tell me everyone on post was watching her but you." Marcus looked intrigued. "So what happened? Did this girl want you because you didn't want her or something? Was she a friend of grandmas or something from her Ziegfeld days?" Marcus rattles off options as they come to him.

"Can I tell the story kid?" Marcus clamps his mouth shut audibly. Luis grins.

"As I was saying… My neck hurt. So I finished up as quickly as I could and stood up. I was at the back of the chow hall and if you get trapped back there when the rush to leave hits it could take twenty minutes or so and I didn't want to be in close proximity to that girl one more minute than I had too."

"Anyway, I stood up and just as I did, the girl stands up too. We are face to face making eye contact across a crowded room of close to one hundred people or more. It was electric. I felt like I was going to die right there. I stood there long enough for Red to ask me. "Whatcha doin dummy? Are ya stayin or are ya goin?"

"I never looked away from her, I just said, "I'm going…to get married… To that girl right there."

Red looked across the room in the direction I was staring and stated loudly. "Married huh? Good luck with that. She aint gonna have nothin' to do with you. You are the most borin' person I ever met." All the guys grunted agreement. By all accounts they were right. I was boring, at least to them. I didn't go out gambling or drinking. I never went to the topless reviews. I just kept to myself and read a lot of the classics; I tell you…I was able to relate to old Heathcliff from Wuthering Heights. I would also ingest whatever sports statistics I could find."

"At any rate, I finally got over myself and went to talk to her. It was one of my finest moments in male terms. I walked up to her, we stared in each other's eyes for what seemed like years and she threw her arms around my neck and kissed me! Hard and long and I kissed her back with all the years of agony and loss I had been holding in my heart."

Marcus had mixed emotions about this. He wasn't sure how to feel. Happy that his grandfather made a connection that possibly wasn't Janie, confused that maybe it was Janie, anxious that the story seemed never ending and somewhat disgruntled that his grandfather had given into temptation, if that is what Luis was saying. "Wait, was that…?"

Luis ignores the interjection, "We could have gotten in trouble for public displays of affection in uniform but neither of us gave a damn. Honestly, it was probably the only moment in my life where every man I knew wanted to be me. All those G.I.'s on base and she chose me. I don't mind bragging, but the joke was on them." Luis's voice cracks as the tears well in his eyes.

"We were finally together Marcus. That day marked five years and eight months since the day we met the first time in the church." Luis's eyes are watery as he finishes his thought. "We walked out of the chow hall and were never apart again, excluding deployments, until she passed. We got married in a small chapel on base a few weeks later, moved into base housing and had our first two children at Ft. Huachuca."

"The day we got married Janie had brought her bible to the church and instructed the base Chaplain to give it to me before the wedding. When he handed it to me I found inside a single rose pressed in the pages and tied to the silk ribbon, bookmark that came inside was my grandmothers promise ring." Luis shakes his head to avoid the welling of tears that had threatened him so many times in the last few days. "I cried when I saw that she had kept it. Just as she cried when I had my best man hand her that ring and the diamond I had recently bought for her encased in the pocket square that held her kiss."

Although Luis was not finished with the story Marcus felt the finality of it in the moment he envisioned in his head. A small wedding without family with just the two witnesses, one for Janie, one for Luis and the Chaplain. It was so moving that Marcus too felt a lump in his throat and emotions threatening to overwhelm him.

"We had a long and happy life together. She never changed or aged a day in all the years we shared. If she did, I didn't notice. She was and still is the girl from this photo. There is an old Nuhuatl word… It is what my father called my mother…Zyanya… It means; Always. If I could have renamed your grandmother I would have named her that. *Always*...I remain in love with her and I *always* will."

Luis holds up the worn photo that had been on the end table. Marcus takes it from his hand and looks into the eyes of the beautiful stranger looking back at him.

It is like the photographer had accidentally captured Janie in the midst of telling her deepest most passionate secret. She was truly captivating in that moment and Marcus can see why this photo was the one Luis chose to carry with him.

"She told me that she hadn't wanted to take her Basic photo because she knew it was going to be ghastly compared to the professional photos that she was accustomed too. When the photographer told her to smile she had asked him sardonically, "What is there to smile about?" And the photographer had said, "Think of the love of your life honey." When she smiled that secret smile she was thinking of me. That is why it is my favorite. In that moment I was there with her, in her heart and you can see it." Marcus nods in agreement.

"You certainly can. Her expression is so deeply private and intimate." He is moved as he returns the photo to his grandfather's loving hands.

"It is a decision Marcus." Luis clears the emotion from his throat. "To love someone like that. It isn't something that happens to you. It is something that you take on. You wear that love like a cape. You let it shield you from the elements and the ugliness of the world. You decide to let it make you a better man. Then you share that cloak with your future wife." Luis says with firm resolve.

Marcus nods again, unable to speak, his throat constricted with emotion. Swallowing several times he speaks, "I guess I have a lot to do tomorrow. Time to turn in old man?" Marcus helps Luis rise from the low deck chair then waits for him to settle into bed before he makes a quiet exit.

Contemplating where he will begin to look for Detective Denis in the morning, Marcus walks lazily across the parking lot to his truck. As he reaches for his truck door a large imposing shape detaches from the shadowy bushes.

-34-
Signs

Isadora returns from the bathroom resigned to her fate, she shuffles half-heartedly back into the room, bumping roughly into Detective Denis. She has changed her whole attitude based on the one statement that Maizer had made. "That boy you met, Marcus, they will kill him too." The simple act of saying his name had the effect of ice water in her face. *It is selfish of me to want to stay if it could involve him and put him in danger. I have to leave. I have to protect him. He is the only real thing I have known in my adult life. If I can't be with him… that is ok. At least I will know he exists and the possibility of that kind of connection exists for me as well.*

Isadora signs the necessary documents, is given a new identity and packed onto a small plane with an unknown location and flown from an unmarked airfield. She doesn't know what awaits her. Only that she is for the first time in her life demolished. She had heard the word devastated over and over in her life and had never truly understood the concept of what it meant. She had cried with every tear she had in her body when they had told her that her brother David Rodrigo Aragon had died of a pulmonary embolism after he had been shot in FBI protection on the courthouse steps of the Cali trial. He was her only family and they had struggled to make something of themselves their whole lives, only for him to die at age thirty six, trying to do the right thing.

Isadora knows pain, she knows loss but never before had she felt an anguish so deep that even her hope is bleeding to death inside her. That is what hurt so much. She is losing hope.

When she had seen Marcus that first time in the Cafeteria she had been struck by an undefinable awareness of him. From that first moment she felt in orbit around him. Then they spoke and she was so excited and pleased that she teased and flirted like she had never done before with anyone else. She would have put on a clown nose and blown up balloons for everyone in the hospital just to feel the warmth of his smile. In that smile she saw her future. She saw kids and rushing home from the hospital to meet him and cook dinner together. She saw every quaint scene from every romantic movie she had ever seen… starring them.

At the time she considered it corny. At the time she had thought they had time to discover all of that. But now…now she felt nothing but isolation and there was no future. Unless… Unless that one tiny ray of sunshine happened, but she couldn't see it through her haze of misery and the fog of unfairness she was wallowing in. She didn't ever want to come in contact with another human being again. If she couldn't have Marcus, then she didn't want to ever fall in love. She didn't want to ever feel close to someone, to something, to a dream, ever again.

Isadora cries silently for hours on the plane, trying to recall his scent, grateful for the loud sounds of the engine and the slight turbulence that keeps everyone in their seats, away from her. Just before she falls asleep she is thinking of that kiss in the parking lot and how she had felt truly alive for the first time in her life. More alive even than when she had been scared for her life. Rubbing her full lips against the back of her hand as she grips a pillow to her face, wishing she would never wake up unless it was to Marcus's face.

When she awakens it is to the jolt of the landing gear making contact with the ground. She is disappointed wryly that they hadn't all died in the air. Her throat feels raw and her eyes feel like someone had poured sand in them while she slept. She sits up, setting the soggy pillow on the seat beside her. She must have cried even in her sleep because the pillow was heavy with spent tears and her whole body felt dehydrated.

She can hear the sounds of the agents and flight staff, gathering their belongings to deplane. Sighing deeply she begins to fold her blanket as she has no possessions to worry about. Her life, her clothes, her furniture, her flat that she loved, her job, her car and her few friends were all left behind. She would just disappear and no one would be the wiser. She was to become a missing person. Her future was to become no one, again.

-35-
Basic Addition

Marcus jumps, putting his hands up ready to fight.

The sunrise breaks over the horizon barely illuminating the dark figure in front of him. The tall person is silhouetted from behind, shadowing their face from Marcus's view. *It could be a Sasquatch and I wouldn't know it.*

"Hey, who is that?" Marcus asks trying to shade his face. Taking a quick sidestep to put the sun at his left he recognizes Uncle Ricky. "Hey, what are you up too? You startled me."

Ricky lifts his gaze to Marcus's face and he can see that something is wrong. Ricky looks both nervous and uncomfortable. "Uh Marcus, you been with dad all night?"

Marcus nods, a knot of disquiet forming in his stomach. "Yeah, we had a few drinks and shared some stories, what's up?" Marcus looks around trying to gather his thoughts. "Were you waiting here for me? Why didn't you come to the room?" Taking a step forward, he reaches for Ricky's arm but misses. "Is everything alright with Lauren?" Marcus takes his phone out of his pocket. It is dead.

Ricky shifts from foot to foot like a kid in trouble then squares up. "Kellan came looking for you earlier when you didn't answer your phone. There was some sort of break-in at the hospital, he saw it on the news… Your girl Marcus, no one has seen her since she left you in the hallway. Her office was destroyed and no one can get ahold of her." Marcus frowns out of confusion but it must have looked like worry.

"Don't worry. The police already confirmed your whereabouts with Kevin. You were at his house with him and the kids during the break in. No one suspects you." Marcus frowns again harder, this time it hurts the muscles of his face. He tries to relax his face and to clear his mind. *Did I drink that much tequila?* He says, "What the hell is going on?" As he thinks, *I saw that cop after Kevin's house. It sounds like he is reassuring me that I am in the clear, like I needed an alibi. This doesn't add up.*

"Uh, wait, my dad… Where is he? Can I use your phone? I need to go to the police station, did they leave info to contact them at Kevin's house? How long have you been waiting here? What the hell?" The rapid barrage of questions leaves Ricky stammering, uncertain of what to answer first. He hands his phone to Marcus.

Marcus dials Kellan's number manually, surprised when his contact information comes up as saved in Ricky's phone. Frowning again he waits for an answer. "Yeah, dad it's Marcus I know you are asleep, I am coming to you… Yeah, I just found out, Ricky is here with me, my phone is dead… No, no, I can sleep later. See you in a bit."

"Marcus hands the phone back to Ricky, hugs him, "Thanks for waiting for me Unc. That had to be miserable. I appreciate it." Jumps into his truck and leaves tire tracks in the hotel parking lot.

Vaulting from his truck Marcus hits the pavement at a run in front of Kevin's house. It seems like he has been doing nothing but dramatically entering and exiting every moment of his life for the last week.

Starting with the call from Kevin, Marcus feels like he has been running on high octane fuel ever since. He considers the possibility of health complications from long term stress as he jogs up the drive but shrugs them off as he enters the house. Kellan is in the kitchen at the table, Kevin is making coffee. "Where are the kids?" Marcus asks.

"Still asleep as I would be if this old coot hadn't woke me up when you called. It is barely six." Marcus cringes.

"Sorry, I was with Luis, finishing up some lose ends. Wanted to get it all wrapped up before I went back to Vegas." He hugs Kellan as he stands up to fix his coffee.

"Well, you smell like tequila and look like hell so I hope Luis is still alive, scotch and tequila in one night?" Kellan holds Marcus at arm's length giving him the once over. "What were you two doing?" Kellan pulls him in and bangs Marcus roughly on the back in teasingly gruff hug.

Marcus shrugs, releasing himself from his father's grip to get his own coffee. "Just talking about the old days. Tell me what happened earlier, after I left. The police showed up?"

Kevin scratches his shiny pate in contemplation. "Yeah, it was the weirdest thing. Two Detectives show up and ask me a bunch of questions about you and where you have been, have I seen your girl with you, did I know her, did you know her well, etc. They had a lot of questions that seemed serious but I swear Marcus, they seemed bored. Like they weren't really interested in what I had to say."

Marcus settles at the table across from Kellan, inhaling deeply, grateful for the warm comforting aroma of the Peruvian Medium roast in his mug. Sipping he considers what Kevin had said. "This coffee is great Kevin, really smooth, thanks. I need it." Kevin smiles fondly.

"Lauren's choice, you know how she is about coffee and tea. I just assume chew Folgers grounds but she wouldn't hear of it, ya know?" Marcus can tell that Kevin is happily less worried about Lauren's condition.

"Tell you the truth… I have been so worried about my wife and kids and what would happen to us, it is a relief to have someone else's drama to worry about." Kevin salutes Marcus in a good natured manner.

The three men discuss at length the visit with the Detectives and what it all could mean. Marcus doesn't know why but he doesn't tell them about seeing Detective Denis at the hospital, but he is certain that what Denis had said was true. "She is unhurt." There was something earnest and sincere about

Detective Denis that told Marcus in his gut that Denis hadn't lied.

The Detectives that had come to speak to Kevin were not Denis, it had been two others and from the description they sounded more official than police. Marcus was beginning to wonder if they really were police at all. It made him feel apprehensive in both his mind and somewhere deep in his navel.

"Did they leave contact information?" Marcus asks. "I think I will just offer to talk to them in case I know something they didn't think to ask. I am worried about Isadora but I *feel* like she is ok. I just think I would know is something was really wrong."

"Yeah?" Kevin asks, skeptical, "How's that? You two have only known each other for two days. Did you partake of the Vulcan Mind Meld or something and didn't tell us?" Marcus's brows knit together at the negativity. Instantly reminded why he has never truly warmed to Kevin.

Kevin looks at Marcus's glower and back peddles, "I'm just asking… how close could your bond possibly be? Lauren and I were together for almost eight months before I knew that she took cream in her coffee, and you can just *feel* if this girl is safe or not?" Kevin rolls his eyes, clearly not understanding, or not wanting to believe.

"Kevin, remind me not to ask you for marriage advice in future." He winks at his brother-in-law, "Maybe you should pay closer attention to my sister." With that, Marcus rinses his cup and sits back down. Kevin stares at the floor, no response available.

Kellan clears his throat loudly to break the silence, a slight grin of pride on his face. "So Marcus, it is almost eight o'clock. Are you heading to the police station?"

"Yes, here in a bit; I need to shower, is that ok with you? Or do you need the bathroom?" Marcus asks Kevin. Kevin shakes his head that he doesn't.

When Marcus returns to the kitchen Kevin is on the phone with Lauren at the hospital. It sounds private so Marcus removes his phone from the charger and looks around the house for Kellan or the kids. It is nearly ten so Marcus is in a hurry to get to the police station.

Finding his father watching the original Star Wars with the kids piled on top of him in the TV room. Marcus forehead kisses everyone goodbye without a word, as this was the easiest way to get his point across without causing a disturbance. Kellan's eyes flutter as though he is trying hard not to fall asleep. Marcus laughs remembering all the times Kellan had looked just like that when he and Lauren were small and in his lap.

Sadness crosses his features as he thinks of Isadora and the loss of hope that Kellan would one day be buried under their children as well. "Can't give up hope yet..." He mumbles beneath his breath as he motions toward his watch for Kellan, indicating he has to go but hopes to return by two pm.

-36-
Bait

Marcus scans the street as he takes his time to unlock his truck manually. He has the uncanny feeling that someone is watching him and tries to look innocuous as he looks for the cause.

At the very end of the street, the opposite end from Kevin and Lauren's house there is a dark SUV with figures that look like people in the front seats. Marcus wants to make excuses in his head thinking they might be waiting for someone to come out of one of the other homes on the street, but the engine isn't on and the homes near the SUV seem quiet.

Marcus slides into the front seat and looks at the SUV in his rear view mirror, starting his engine he pulls away from the curb slowly, to see if the SUV starts their engine. Marcus speaks to himself aloud. "I'm just paranoid; if they are following me, they will be following me to the police station, let them." He shrugs and decides to get on with his day.

Marcus is just starting to let go of the feeling of being watched when he exits the housing development only to notice an official looking sedan with two suited gentlemen and many aerial antenna, shuffle around and start their car as he drives by them. The suited man in the passenger seat makes eye contact with Marcus as their vehicles pass. They are not trying to be covert. Without question *those* two men had been waiting for him.

Marcus looks for an excuse to stop and locates a gas station only two blocks from the police station. He pulls up to a pump and methodically goes through the motions to get gas, keeping his eye out for the sedan. It passes by slowly, both men looking hard at Marcus. He sees the sedan park amongst squad cars at the far end of the block diagonally from the Police station. "They must be cops." Marcus reasons aloud, less nervous about their presence.

As Marcus returns to the clerk for his change, the SUV pulls up next to Marcus's truck. Having forgotten about it due to the presence of the sedan, Marcus walks around the front of the SUV about to get into his truck when the two hulking olive skinned men exit their vehicle with menacing purpose. Just as they lay hands on Marcus the two suited men from the sedan pull up, tires screeching as another duplicate sedan pulls up behind the SUV, blocking them in. Four agents close in on them before the two thugs have a chance to run.

The entire scene goes silent in Marcus's head, he just stands there stunned as the men with guns surround them and drag the other two men to the ground at gunpoint, cuff them and gruffly shove them into the sedans. He feels like he is in the eye of a tornado as the world whirls around him, chaos and danger just an arm's length away. Someone grabs him by the arm roughly before his sense of surreal silence recedes, leaving him with the impression of walking out of a hearing test booth, complete with the residual ringing in his ears.

Suddenly and overwhelmingly all the sound comes crashing back around him. He looks at the man holding his arm as he finishes a sentence Marcus was just now registering, "that won't be too much trouble will it Mr. McGregor?"

The sound of his last name shocks him into reality. Immediately it occurs to Marcus that these people know him on a level that he couldn't begin to understand. "Uh, I'm sorry, I missed most of that. Could you repeat it please?"

"My name is Special Agent Jones. I am with the FBI. I will be briefing you if that won't be too much trouble." The tall light skinned black man says to him politely. "I will let go of you if you just follow me please." Marcus nods and Agent Jones releases his arm. Marcus follows him to a dark sedan looking back as another agent pulls out of the gas station in his own truck. Marcus frowns unable to remember when they had taken his keys from him.

The entire scenario had taken less than ten minutes Marcus realizes as he looks at his watch. Acknowledging that he must be suffering from sensory overload, Marcus shakes his head feeling like hours of time had lapsed. Agent Jones begins to speak and Marcus listens raptly without interruption.

"As you may already be aware, Ms. Trevino is missing. We had suspected that the men, who nearly accosted you, were going to attempt to do so. We do not currently know why you were a target specifically; only that it must be connected to Ms. Trevino's disappearance. Now that we have these men we are hoping to find out their level of involvement. We believe they are part of a group that targets couples. We had reason to believe that you and Ms. Trevino had been targeted at the Hospital as we had been following these men for several days. I am not at liberty to tell you what their operation consists of, only that taking them into custody will help us end their crimes." He continues on repeating the same information in several different ways when Marcus begins to feel like he is being drowned in information that is no information at all.

He begins to watch the Agent more than listening to him, coming to the conclusion that it is all smoke and mirrors. The disingenuous micro facial expressions combined with the repetition implants doubt in Marcus's heart and mind. Over and over he is "briefed" by three different Agents only to be told exactly what Agent Jones had told him in the car.

They fed him cold sandwiches and asked him very little as they already seemed to know everything about him. One of the Agents even had a file with a picture of him and Isadora talking in front of the hospital. He had only gotten a glimpse of the picture; her in that beautiful sundress, looking like a gorgeous figment of his imagination, before the only Agent in a grey suit had snapped the folder closed.

Marcus has a headache and is surprised to see it is dark when he is escorted from the official FBI building he hadn't remembered entering. Signing for his keys, phone and wallet, like a common criminal being released from jail, Agent Jones escorts Marcus to a private parking lot to retrieve his truck.

Marcus gets into his truck, asks for directions to the freeway and makes his way out of the parking lot. As he drives back to Kevin's house in the silence of his truck interior one clear thought immerges from his clouded mind. "I have no idea what happened today. I have no idea because they wanted me to have no idea. The whole point of today was to confuse and beguile me and it worked. The police never had anything to do with this."

Marcus pulls up to Kevin's house tired and exhausted. Leaning his forehead on the steering wheel he allows the curtain of sadness and loss to lower over his heart. He is finally realizing that he will never see her again. No matter what happened to her, she is gone and he is helpless to do anything about it. He feels now exactly like he felt sitting in that waiting room waiting to hear that Lauren was going to die, only three days ago. It felt like a lifetime ago and yet like a dream.

Marcus clenches his fists and pounds on the dashboard to either side of the steering wheel. He is about to yell and scream like a mad man when a sharp, forceful clicking sound on his window startles him. Detective Denis is knocking on his window with what looks like a phone.

Marcus turns the keys in the ignition to turn on the electric windows. The low whirring sound stops before Detective Denis says anything.

Looking up and down the street guiltily, Denis tries to hand Marcus the phone. "She wanted you to have this. I have been waiting for you to come back. I saw you leave and the suits follow you. I followed and saw the thing at the gas station. Sorry about all that. No one could have warned you. I am not even supposed to be here. As far as you are concerned Isadora Trevino is a missing person. That is all you are meant to know. But before she disappeared she slipped this to me. She didn't say but I listened to the message. This is for you…" He pushes the phone towards Marcus again. Marcus takes it gingerly from his hand.

Marcus opens his mouth to ask a question but Denis turns in a military style about face, striking out away from the truck, obviously determined to ignore Marcus and leave.

Denis starts his car as lights in the front window of Kevin's house come on.

-37-
Family

Jeff and Kellan rush down the sidewalk to the truck. Marcus slips the phone in his pocket and closes his truck door behind him. He rounds the back of his truck bed, Jeff launches himself into Marcus's arms, tears flowing down his face. Marcus catches him as he clings to Marcus's chest.

Marcus hugs him close. "What's wrong big man? You ok? Is your Mom all right?" Marcus's eye brows rise in question as he makes eye contact with Kellan, Kellan shrugs and taps his watch.

Remembering that he had left the house at mid-morning and promised to return in the early afternoon, Marcus nods.

"Hey buddy, I'm sorry, I got caught up." Marcus begins. Jeff cuts him off sobbing into his neck.

"Grandpa was worried when you didn't come back and he wouldn't talk about it but I could tell because he couldn't sit still and he kept trying to call you." Jeff's voice is muffled but Marcus understands every anguished word.

Marcus sets Jeff gently on the ground and hugs the boy to his chest. "I really am sorry buddy. I … didn't have my phone on me all day. I was kept busy by the police and didn't think of checking my phone. I get it. You have a right to worry. After your mom being sick and now I didn't come back on time. It's too much." Marcus kisses Jeff on the top of his thick mop of hair. "It won't happen again. I promise." Kellan looks stern but curious. Marcus knows he will have to answer some questions.

Marcus pats Jeff on the backside. "Can you find something for me to eat? I am starving." Jeff grins and runs in the house. Kellan and Marcus follow.

Kellan takes a deep breath about to ask questions. Marcus raises his hand to halt the interrogation. "Dad, I am exhausted and my brain is fried. I will tell you everything later. Let me just enjoy tonight with the kids. You get up early tomorrow as well right?" Kellan nods.

"Wake me up when you get up and we will talk. I have to drive back to Vegas tomorrow, an early start would be best." Kellan nods agreement.

The evening is spent watching movies and playing board games with the kids. Marcus enjoys the laughter and it lifts his spirits to hear Cassie's little voice and Jeff's voice crack at high notes, obviously beginning puberty. Everyone seems to be in better moods, no longer worried about Lauren or Marcus. The entire time the phone Detective Denis handed him burns into his thigh.

After Marcus tucks Jeff and Cassie into bed, saying his goodbyes so he won't have to wake them in the morning, he goes to his room and lays down on the bed staring at the ceiling. He doesn't have a good reason for the hesitation, he just isn't sure he wants to know definitively that his fears will be confirmed.

He gets up and paces the room, then thinks to himself, *what would grandpa do?* He has his answer immediately. He opens the phone. The phone has been wiped clean with the exception of one recorded unsent voice note.

Pushing the speaker button Marcus listens with his head in his hands, her voice close to his ear.

"Marcus, I am going to plant this phone on Detective Denis without his knowledge or permission. I can only hope he has compassion enough to pass this on to you. If you are listening Denis… I am asking you please, if you believe in the hope of love at all, please."

"Marcus, I only have a few seconds and I don't know what to tell you. All I know is that I felt something for you that I have never felt for anyone… Ever. I was in the witness protection program when we met. My name isn't Isadora. I can't tell you my real name and I have no idea what it will be now. Don't worry about me, I didn't do anything terrible," She laughs nervously, "and I will be safe. I don't want to open Pandora's Box and run the risk that you will ever look me up and someone somewhere looking for me, trace it back to you. I know this is selfish but I am going to ask you… if you felt anything real between us… don't forget me. I will never forget you. I wish we could have had a future but a past that isn't mine got in the way of that. I can only pray that one day all this will be resolved. If so I will find you… if you can… if you want too… wait for me." She sighs deeply sounding sad and tired before the click of the receiver ends the message.

Marcus looks at the phone, it says palmOne on the face above the screen, has a similar stunted antenna to his own and a broad silver casing. Looking at the phone closer he can see one of the options is a camera. That is new technology and he had just gotten a new phone for that very reason. Isadora, or whatever her name really is, had spent serious money on this phone. He smiles, impressed that she is a gadget person, like he is. Just another aspect of her personality that he wishes he could have known.

Playing with the features of the phone he discovers the photo album. Three pictures of her face taken in succession with little difference indicates that she took them in hurry. He smiles at her beautiful face, holding the phone to his heart as though it is her head, one single tear wells up in his right eye. The small reel of memories he has of her streams through his mind. As he settles on their first sweet kiss in the pudding shop the tear overwhelms the lid and runs down his cheek.

Marcus rises from the bed leaving the phone behind as he gathers his toiletry bag and towel for the walk down the hall. Opening his door just as Kellan was about to knock he catches his father with his fist raised in the air.

"Hey son, you ok? I noticed the light still on under your door. I know you didn't get any sleep last night, you should be sleeping or that drive back tomorrow will be hell."

"I'm ok dad, I am about to shower and head to bed. See you in the morning? You are still waking me up right?"

"Yes, of course... Luis called, I thought you were asleep, so I told him you would call him in the morning. I guess Ricky must have told him what happened at the hospital. He was a little worried, I explained that everything was settled."

Kellan hugs Marcus tight to his chest, smashing the toiletries between them. "Okay, okay Dad, I love you too." Marcus chuckles. "I will leave a note with the hotel for the old man tomorrow.

The water of the shower streams down Marcus's face and neck cleansing him of his pain and doubt. He thinks long and hard about how the last week has altered the course of his life in more ways than he can fathom. He is now in love with a woman he can't have and can't even try to pursue.

He knows that he doesn't want to love anyone else, even though he doesn't even know her name and he knows that he is dually ecstatically happy and dismally sad about the entire situation. He knows that he has her voice and picture to hold onto but he doesn't know how long that will sustain him. He remembers kissing her near her car and the look in her eyes when she spoke to him outside of Lauren's room.

Recalling what Lauren had said he knows that he will do what Isadora asked him. He will wait for her. Not because she asked but because he has no choice. He is after all addicted to the feeling she gave him and he remembers thinking that he would forever be chasing that feeling. "Just because she is gone, *possibly forever,* it doesn't change those feelings." Marcus mumbles to the showerhead, letting the water hit him directly in the face.

Marcus settles into bed and writes a note to Luis before turning off the light.

Grandpa,

You told me it is a decision to stay in love with someone. I will hold onto that thought as I begin the rest of my life without her. I think you were right but I now know that it isn't a decision to love someone in the beginning. It isn't something we choose to do. Love does happen to us... at first... then, we happen to it, as we fall. Then as it goes along... It is the decision to be only with someone who makes you feel like you can fly and not settling for anything less.

Staying in love is the real decision.

Thank you for telling me your story.
Love Always,
Marcus

He turns off the light leaving the note on his nightstand and clicks on the tiny television on the dresser. The local news begins, breaking with a missing person report and a story about the break in at Faith General. Marcus looks up to see Isadora's blurry security badge photo on a missing person's sheet. Exhausted he relaxes into the pillow, vaguely wondering how many strangers will see her beautiful face and look for her in crowds, thinking it is now a less safe neighborhood. Annoyed at the reminder of the deception he closes his eyes and falls into a dreamless sleep.

The next morning Kellan wakes him up before the sun rises. They both shuffle around the house bleary eyed and unhappy until they walk out together locking the door behind them.

Parting ways at the end of the driveway, Kellan hugs Marcus tight. "I will come to Vegas to see you soon Kiddo. Maybe we can talk Kevin and Lauren into bringing the kids. You know you are going to need family…" He trails off not mentioning Marcus's loss.

Marcus is about to say, *it isn't like someone has died,* but realizes that he is the only one that doesn't think Isadora is missing. Kellan and Kevin didn't ask him any pressing questions after the news cast, mistakenly assuming Marcus's sullen attitude was due to her disappearance. He lets them think that. It is just easier. It will keep everyone from curiosity.

"Yeah, for sure, you are always welcome. Drive safe, Reno isn't too far. Call me when you get home and get settled." Kellan agrees, punches Marcus fondly in the shoulder and walks away.

Marcus drops off the note for Luis on his way out of town and is on the I-5 before the sun is fully up. Looking forward to the long drive home in solitude.

Epilogue…

Marcus is just wiping down the counters of the bar as his last day shift employee leaves for the night. He seats himself in the tall leather booth opposite the bar and looks around. A beautiful blonde in tight jeans enters and they make eye contact. Marcus smiles and nods as she smiles a wide perfectly white grin and inclines her head.

Marcus is accustomed to this. It happens every day. Beautiful women make eyes at him but he never encourages anything beyond smiles. He has become something of an urban legend amongst his regular female patrons. Many of them whisper, when they think he cannot hear, that he is gay. He smiles every time he hears it.

He is no-more gay than Bill Clinton. He just hasn't been *struck* as his father had once put it. There hasn't been another single face that has made him pause since *her!* That is how he refers to Isadora in his mind now. He has long since ceased calling her Isadora, as that was never really her name. He just calls her… *HER*.

The blonde looks his direction swinging her mane of tresses over her shoulder, the motion attracting his attention, just as she intends. Marcus walks to his private booth near the huge indoor fire pit, and looks down at his ledger in a clear attempt to ignore her. She frowns prettily but concentrates on her group of companions.

Five years of totaling his till and he still dreads it. He sighs, sipping a finger of scotch, lodging his right hand in his hair as he begins to tap away at his calculator with his left. Glancing up from time to time to watch the news and to rest his eyes. Jon, the ruggedly handsome and shirtless bartender asks him, "Hey boss, you need a refill?" Marcus looks up but waves him away.

He had bought this space on the corner of Boylston St. in Boston six and a half years ago and remodeled it with his own two hands. He put in every booth and carved every rail himself. The fact that he had remodeled it entirely on his own over that time frame became something of a tall bar tale of its own. When he opened the entire street full of his soon to be competition celebrated with him.

His story and the Lonely Griffin made the local news. He had never intended for his remodel to become news worthy, it had originally been intended to be therapy.

Not long after receiving his Masters of Business from UNLV and getting his bar tending license, Marcus had been in a near fatal car accident with a train and a faulty railroad warning system, leaving him with a fancy new prosthetic leg from the calve down and a huge settlement to recover with.

The money was nice and so was all the paid medical care and rehabilitation. He worked towards being able to play basketball and his life had physically returned to normal for the most part. The injury had even helped him get over his depression concerning *her,* but it had been a long hard mental and emotional journey as the tattoos the covered both arms and across his chest could testify. Although he still believed her to be a good person with a good heart he had long ago convinced himself that she wouldn't want him now that he isn't whole. *She probably wouldn't even recognize me.* He thought as he looked at his, shaggy hair and bearded reflection in the canted mirror above the bar.

That thought provided him with the comfort and provocation to start fresh and leave Las Vegas.

He had been watching the real estate market on Boylston St. ever since he had taken a trip to Boston on a college basketball trip. He had known then that he wanted to open his own bar there one day. Never dreaming that it would be any time prior to retirement.

Shortly after he had received his settlement from the accident, this spot had gone on the market and Marcus bought it immediately. The property had been cheap and nearly condemnable.

Still deciphering the days totals, he barely notices as the news anchor updates a months old story concerning some dirt bag that had unsuccessfully tried to murder a girl in Canada and been shot twelve times by the girl he was trying to kill. Apparently he was linked to an old drug cartel and the girl had some kind of hit out on her from some years before. *Serves him right.* Marcus thinks to himself, listening halfheartedly as he totals columns.

Another girl, exceptionally lovely with short dark curls beginning at her collarbone, but lifting high at the nape of her neck, hinting at several tattoos mostly hidden by her flowing tank-top enters the bar but Marcus doesn't make the effort to greet her as he had the blonde. He is too set on his task, and doesn't want to be distracted. This is his least favorite part of owning the bar.

Jon quickly appraises the new entrant immediately noting her obscured face as one he had never seen before. He returns his attention to the news cast. Referring to ethic beauty with waist length curls on the television, Jon states raucously for the men at the bar. "Now *that* is the kind of girl I want to marry. You have got to respect a woman that can handle a gun… it keeps a fella in line ya know?" He laughs heartily encouraging comments from the patrons. Several men make indistinct murmurs in return. Marcus closes his mind to their prattle continuing too grimly tap, tap on the calculator.

"God *damn it*," he curses quietly, noticing a row he had missed. Scrubbing his pencil across the paper as though trying to start a fire; Marcus successfully eradicates both the graphite as well as his last hope of quick completion.

"Maybe you should get an accountant." A pleasantly familiar voice says from a small distance. Still Marcus doesn't look up he just acknowledges the comment.

"Indeed."

He begins on the offending column yet again. The click of the buttons lull him into a hypnotic state of concentration.

A hand enters his field of vision reaching across the table for a phone sitting to his far left. Marcus abandons the figures, immediately infuriated at the audacity, grabbing the girl by the wrist firmly he stands, yelling, "What the hell do you think you are doing?" Everyone in the bar shifts to watch the disturbance.

Marcus looks down into beautiful, smoldering burnt umber eyes for an answer. All anger leaving his body instantaneously. "I came back for my phone." She says.

Marcus crushes her to him in a kiss so brutal it could only be described as beautiful. Everyone in the bar stops to stare. They kiss long and ravenously, kindling the primal longing of every onlooker in the Lonely Griffin.

When they finally break apart they are both breathless and glowing with certainty. "I knew you would have it. This is mine right?" She holds up the battered, barely silver palmOne.

"Yes ma'am it is, so is this." Marcus reaches into his pocket and hands her a tattered napkin. "You are a little late."

Opening the napkin she breathlessly reads aloud as her voice catches, thick with tears of joy.

Meet me in the front lobby at 5:30. Her kiss is still there, barely visible.

www.ingramcontent.com/pod-product-compliance
Lightning Source LLC
Chambersburg PA
CBHW022355040426
42450CB00005B/197